AUSSIE
TRUE
CRIME
STORIES

JOE TOG

FOREWORD

In this compilation of twenty short stories by Joe Tog, the criminal genre is nailed exactly as it was during the 70s and the 80s – he experienced it – both inside prison and on the outside. Step by step he describes how a convicted murderer carried out an audacious escape from Pentridge Prison. An arsonist at work, along with bomb-making and how to morph a gun, are just some of the criminal subjects covered in this book. Card cheating, safe breaking and a street rort, all colourfully detailed as he segues from story to story.

Twice on Interpol's Most Wanted list, Joe Tog escaped from two South Australian prisons as well as two Victorian prisons. Shot twice in the head during a shoot-out with police, his criminal background and willingness to lay bare his personal experiences through factual story-telling combine to give this book a ring of authenticity not usually found in True Crime.

+ + +

CONTENTS

WASTED EFFORT
127
An abnormal environment produces abnormal conduct.

SNIFFER DOGS
163
We are better than we think we are.

DREAMIN'
179
Good intentions falter when temptation appears.

GAMMA RAYS
205
A solution is there if searched for.

GOOD OIL
223
Dogs really are our best friends.

ARSON
231
Fire is an uncontrollable beast.

BY MANY MEANS
239
Where there is a will, there is a way.

1
FIVE-CARD DRAW

A penny-farthing bicycle

LIFE IS SHORT: ADAPT AND MOVE ON!

- Joe Tog

Eric, my mother's regular Tuesday night card-playing friend, was quite old compared to me: at least 50 to my 23. Whippet in build and not overly tall, he sported a bristly moustache and wore John Lennon glasses. He displayed a friendly disposition to all he met, showing a character full of charm and bonhomie; the genuine article back then in the late 70s – old school. Courteous to a fault, he always wore a tie, and was helpful in every way. My mum, constantly out to improve me, suggested he was a good example for me to model myself on.

I suspected he had ulterior motives towards my mother, at first, which made me wary and even a little aggressive towards him;

but after sitting down and enjoying a few of my mother's home-cooked meals with him, and afterwards a friendly game of canasta, I thought Eric was a *'what you see, is what you get'* type of person. He always arrived with a block of Cadbury's chocolate and a bottle of tawny port, and left any remaining unfinished portions for mum. I recognised him from around the traps, but never broached it with him in front of mum. Encounters at gambling dens – all illegal in those days – might have slanted Eric adversely in my mother's mind.

Police controlled illegal gaming in central Melbourne: baccarat, two-up, and manila, but throughout the outer suburbs were a multitude of impromptu home games of poker beyond the ability of gaming police to get a handle on. I preferred and frequented those games because the odds of winning were not pure chance, and watching the piles of ready cash on the table in front of each player change hands was exciting. (There was no such thing as casino-chips in those days of *'grab your cash and run'* in the event of a gaming-squad police raid.) Some homes were so organised and had police protection, that a dedicated dealer dealt the cards while the home-owner skimmed 5% from every pot. Provided the betting limit was fixed and reasonable, I liked to play. That is where I recognised Eric; in smoky rooms seated at card tables, often playing with the high rollers while others, like me, watched on and dreamed.

It was not long before I again encountered him at a game, only this time we greeted each other and were on talking terms while waiting for seats at a table to become available. Without my mother's presence to dampen our conversation, we spoke easily and openly discussed the pros and cons of gambling. Probing each other's poker knowledge, I very quickly learned that Eric had a phenomenal skill when it came to calculating hands of cards and had probably forgotten more about the odds of poker than I could ever know. He opened up a bit more, explaining that I should take care this night because Yugoslavs operated this particular house and criminals circulated amongst them.

I asked, "Why are you here?" thinking that what he had warned me of was nothing special. All gambling places attract a variety of seedy people to them. His laconic answer said it all: "Money, son." He beamed a smile after saying it.

I figured that was a fair enough reason and changed the conversation to cover my obviously limited knowledge on the subject. His character had undergone a subtle shift and clearly hardened, no longer like the soft person who visited mum, and I felt slightly perplexed by his change. I attributed his toughened attitude to psyching up for the coming game.

There were three tables operating in this house, one in each bedroom. Eventually two players at the poker table we were watching pulled out of the game and left. Eric grabbed the back of a seat and before sitting said, "They bet big on this table and I intend to take some home with me". He quickly filled the vacant seat as I sat on the other, with him suggesting that I should wait for a spot at a low-stakes table.

Perhaps I should point out now, looking back over the years, I have always been an average player; but back when ignorance was bliss, I believed I was shit-hot. This was the first time I had joined a high-stakes game, but thought I was up to it. Eric's quiet confidence had misled me into believing that I could be as good at poker as he was.

A variety of poker games exist: the one I prefer (and which I sat at) deals out five cards face down where you keep the cards you want and discard the rest. A round of bets based on the cards held advances to the next stage in the game, when a second round of cards are dealt to again bring your hand up to five cards. It now becomes serious business with bets and bluffs, and counter-bets growing ever higher until called and the pot won with winning cards, or lose that particular round.

Into the game a half-hour playing against five others and I had held my losses to a few hundred dollars when finally four cards came my way that I could certainly win on: five of hearts, four of hearts, three of hearts, two of hearts, and a four of spades which I instantly discarded. With seven hundred dollars of betting money on the table in front of me (I had arrived with one thousand) with an open-ended straight flush in my hand, I had *two* chances of filling the straight with *one* draw card: an ace at the bottom, or a six at the top. Only a higher straight or a flush could beat me – no other poker hand could – so a loss seemed *very* unlikely.

Up until then I had watched Eric's style of play. Contrary to what he had said in our earlier conversation regarding his poker acumen he acted dithery and undecided in some of his betting. However, I put that down to manipulation of the other players by sending false 'tells' and winning cleverly. I noticed also that he was the only one at the table who consistently slid his winnings into a pocket so that the moderate stack of cash beside him never varied in size. I challenged him a few times to up the ante, but he simply threw his hand in, without even risking a small wager to learn if my style of play relied on bluffs.

The card dealt to me was an ace of hearts. My pulse raced with excitement. I had drawn the bottom end of a straight flush! My face shortly froze; I hoped it had not told all that I was on a winner. I sucked in a controlled breath before throwing two fifties on top of the pile of cash building in the table centre and saying as casually as possible, "I'm in for a hundred". I looked at Eric.

He threw his cards in, shaking his head, and my first thought was that I had overacted my nonchalance in betting too big to begin the second round in the hope of drawing in other punters' money. Yet, his headshake to me was more than a rueful gesture of loss, though others at the table would have read it as such. It was a definite *No*, so I watched him, wondering what he meant.

Again, he slowly shook his head while dropping his eyes to my cards, indicating he was saying no to them. I ignored him and watched the others ante up, knowing the next bet for me to stay in the game would exceed five hundred. I again took a quick glance at Eric.

He pulled his collar in a peculiar way – a coded gesture used by criminals to warn an associate to be wary – showing he knew of my darker activities and that he was *au fait* and serious. It shocked me! After that, he had my full attention.

Leaning forward to conceal his action, the fingers of his right hand spread open against his chest as he nodded towards my cards, followed by both of his hands showed briefly with thumbs hidden, before indicating with a nod towards the player opposite me. I sat thunderstruck. In only a few seconds of clever gesture Eric had told me my hand correctly, and what could only be the hand of my opponent, an eight high straight flush.

Trying to consider my options clearly and aware that all of my money would be forfeited if I lost, in a thrall of indecision I folded mentally and threw my cards in. Eric removed his glasses and proceeded to polish them with a large handkerchief as though he had not a care in the world. My heart thumped, convinced that I had misread everything and thrown away a superb hand for nothing.

Normally a winner is under no obligation to show their cards if an opponent folds (to conceal if they were bluffing). Additionally, a folded hand seen is bad play (those still in the game can recalculate odds based on cards seen). In this case, the winner, challenged to show the winning hand before claiming the very large pot, did so: an eight high, just as Eric had gestured. My enthusiasm petered out after that and not long afterwards, I withdrew from the game, hoping that Eric would do the same so we could talk. Annoyingly, he remained firmly seated, and played on.

A fortnight later, I again visited my mum for her Tuesday roast and, as expected, Eric turned up for dinner with his chocolate and port in hand. We talked about sport but never mentioned the subject of gambling. When dinner was done, during the minutes it took for mum to clear the plates and set the card table up for canasta, we agreed on a place to meet the following day. For me the card game that evening was lacklustre and went far too long. I was gone before ten o'clock.

+ + +

The beer garden at the River Inn was packed and noisy, a perfect place to meet someone. Eric sipped on a large shandy while I downed a pot of VB and, after having dispensed with the trivia, I tackled the facts.

"How did you know what cards I held; and why help me at risk to yourself?" Both those questions needed answers for me to move on.

"It was a matter of principle; knowing your mother and all. They fed you that ace, son. Your confidence would have borrowed to back that hand, and put you in debt to them." He nodded all the while he spoke.

"No I wouldn't have, I wouldn't have borrowed!" I blustered, unhappy with his assessment, knowing that was *exactly* what I would have done. "And how can you say they cheated?"

"I know them, not personally, and that's why I was there. Two can play at that game." Again, he just nodded.

"I don't get it? How did you know my hand?"

"I cheated just like them." This time he refrained from nodding, but stared at me, tapping his temple instead. It took a moment for what he admitted to register.

"How did you?" I demanded, and then added, "Was the whole table in on it?"

"No; only two, but they were good. The dealer beside me fed the one opposite you."

I persisted: "How did you do it?"

"Does it matter?"

"I never *saw* anything," I frustratingly snapped.

"And they didn't notice anything either, because they weren't looking. So full of their own need to fleece the cashed-up newbie, they missed me completely."

Changing tack, exposed as a novice, I asked, "Did they get you?"

"No likelihood of that, son. I strolled with eight hundred and most of it theirs."

It pleased me to hear that he had hit their pocket, because I hated the bastards for targeting me. I left Eric out of my anger response; he had saved both my money and my pride.

A few beers later, he handed me a used deck of cards, which I took and shuffled, expecting that perhaps I was about to be shown a thing or two on gambling. Eric did give me a lesson, but not the kind I originally imagined.

"You've shuffled them enough," he said. "Give me the deck." After doing as told, he dealt five cards face down to each of us.

I picked up my cards and sorted through them confirming, by asking, if the game was five-card draw. He nodded and advised that I should hold the pair of nines in my hand and discard the other three cards. Before I could finish exclaiming, "How do you know – before I know – what I've got?", he added a rider: "The next card coming to you is a nine."

When dealt it *was* a nine, along with a pair of fours. Nevertheless, the hand I held was good: a full house is okay. I asked what he had, expecting him to pick up his cards and sort them.

Eric progressed through them face down on the table; touching each card, he rattled off its suit and value. *Very* impressive, and to cap it off he again told me what the next card would be off the deck. I grabbed it up and sure enough, it was as he said.

Obviously, each card was marked in such a way that it told him: but after intense study of the deck, I gave up, admitting defeat. (If what you are seeking is unknown, how do you know when you find it?) There were no fingernail marks or faint colour stains from make-up, the two commonest ways of marking an active deck.

The back of each card portrayed a man wearing black knickerbockers with a plaid vest, sporting a trilby, pedalling down a country lane seated high on the frame of a nineteenth century penny-farthing bicycle. The picture of this weird contraption filled the entire card. (Imagine a bike with a two-metre high front wheel, and a half-metre rear wheel with the rider precariously seated high above the rear wheel.)

Eric placed a fingertip on a card in front of me, indicating the small rear wheel. "There are four spokes, each assigned a suit: heart, diamond, club, and spade. This card's third spoke is broken; a club." I went to grab it, to check if he was correct, but he stopped me with a curt, "Wait till I finish, son."

He continued: "The large wheel has thirteen spokes and this one's fifth spoke is broken." This time he gave a slight bob of his head to indicate now I should pick it up and confirm its face.

It was exactly as he said — a five of clubs! I immediately flipped the card over to peer more closely at its back. Yet as hard as I concentrated, knowing the truth stared me in the face, I still could not discern the deceit! Half a dozen spokes, besides the fifth one on the large wheel, had small gaps in them as though slight imperfections had occurred during printing. According to that evidence, any number of card values could have been it. I methodically compared the other cards in front of me, confirming that most of the spokes had random breaks in them caused naturally during the print run. Then I made the connection.

No breaks were close to the *tyre rim* on any of the cards *except* for the ones correlating to the denomination on the face: I finally understood the key.

"How did you mark them, though?" I asked in wonder, having already held a few cards up to the light. "The plastic finish is still perfect."

"Leftovers from the mafia days in Havana after Castro closed the casinos and kicked them out of Cuba," he coolly stated. (Inferring they were manufactured that way in a print shop.)

"So that's it," I sighed, accepting his explanation as to how he turned the table on the Yugoslavs.

He had convinced me . . . almost.

"Hang on!" I exclaimed. "We played with Numeros, not this Penny Farthing kind."

Eric chuckled, and then said, "The principle's the same. Different cards were used, that's all."

"Yeah, I get your point," I conceded. "But why did you finally show me? You didn't have to."

"An idea has risen to mind, on which we could both profit." He lent towards me and began to impart his idea.

+ + +

POSTSCRIPT:

Eric acted proactively by sending everyone he knew gift packs of Penny Farthings and Numero cards for Christmas, Easter, weddings, a birthday, but mostly to strangers (especially those who hosted poker nights). Even I received a deck on-gifted by my mother, prior to Eric and I joining forces to skim some of the black money laundered through illegal gambling. The Numero deck I owned underwent greater wear by me searching to unravel the secret they held, than they ever could if used in a hundred games of poker.

Over and over and over, I handled that deck of Numero cards, studied both near to the nose and at arm's length, hoping to divine their key. They were not marked and not interfered with in any way, I was certain. The card faces were standard for a deck, white background with black and red values. The back appeared bland. Having a light-blue background peppered with black and green numbers of every value, size, and font, the scheme blended so well that the visual effect appeared as a swirl of muted colour.

Eventually, however, by studying the entire deck of fifty-four cards (two jokers) laid out face down in a block and continually rearranging them, I discovered the back of each card had an association to the relationship of those kaleidoscopic numbers, with miniscule variation, confirming to my satisfaction that each deck was cut from one large sheet. These playing cards, printed akin to a sheet of money at the mint, were individually unique. Was it purely coincidental that the backing for the cards was an entire picture, so to speak? Did Eric decipher and eventually memorise fifty-four individual patterns and mentally assign each back of a card to the face value of which it belonged?

Even in the mahogany room of Melbourne's Crown Casino where poker is strictly controlled and presumed honest, without marked cards to help, Eric would have been a poker player the equal of Joe Hasham. (An extraordinarily clever Australian poker player who beat the arse off the Americans at their own game, a few years back, and brought home more than two million dollars in winnings.)

Who knows . . .?

+ + + +

2
ARTFUL

Vermeer: girl with a pearl earring

PROGRESS ALWAYS INVOLVES RISK

During one of those days in prison when the hours crawl by and boredom sets in, Les told a few others and me about a scam he and two of his mates pulled on a Melbourne insurance company.

When talking, Les had the habit of looking directly into your eyes, and sometimes it disconcerted his listener. If you didn't know him you could be forgiven for thinking he felt aggressive towards you. Unlike his two stockier brothers, he was tall and slim, which may have led some to believe he was a pushover. Think again!

I only ever saw him fight once – total aggression, and unstoppable, until his opponent lay comatose on the concrete at his feet. Everyone who watched him learnt a salutary lesson that day: always err on the side of caution when assessing an opponent.

Being a well-known and respected criminal by his peers, Les knew that his notoriety was an asset but had no way to apply it gainfully to put money in his pocket. A bit similar to his being a competent fighter; but without a professional bout involving stake-money, what value was it? Les searched fruitlessly for a solution to his dilemma until one day a crooked detective approached him with a proposal.

The detective promised Les that he could build up credit on the books (if ever arrested in the future) by helping him to identify a cat burglar known to have stolen valuable family heirlooms from wealthy business people in the St Kilda area. It was unstated, but obviously a large kickback would go to the detective if successful. Les told him very clearly what he should do with his insulting offer. And as far as Les remembers, only a few articles of jewellery were ever recovered.

However, that encounter had sowed a seed of thought that gradually grew to fruition in the shape of a plan based on the commonly known fact that art galleries where valuable paintings are on public display always, always, insured their works. In addition, he knew there were insurance companies who specialised in indemnifying artwork.

Every ambitious criminal steered clear of stealing art, unless an avid collector offered a bounty beforehand, because the easy recognition and controlled market weighed heavily on the side of capture. In addition though, as a hidden corollary, that inside knowledge allowed security in the field of art to be notoriously slack.

While his two associates searched for a likely target, he diligently watched and followed, one by one, the staff of an insurance office in Melbourne until he located a bistro-bar where a few went for lunch and a Friday drink together before knocking off for the weekend. Les developed a nodding acquaintance with two of them.

A month further down the track, six paintings disappeared out of fourteen on display in a boutique Sydney gallery. The leading detective on the case went public immediately. He stated the following: "These art thieves were professional and knew exactly what they wanted. We suspect the pieces will go to an overseas buyer." The insurance on the six stolen paintings exceeded five hundred thousand dollars (equivalent to two million in 2013).

Les was at the bistro the following day to eavesdrop on whatever slipped off the tongues of the unwary and worried insurance staff. Unfortunately, he sat unsatisfied through the lunch hour; no one of interest put in an appearance. The next week turned out to be the same. It took a further fortnight of random visits by Les to the small pub, before he could start up a brief conversation with one of the insurance men. And because his face by now had become familiar at the bistro, his target never suspected for a moment that Les had an ulterior motive and had worked assiduously towards this key contact.

The actuary filled a mid-level position in the company, and could therefore make binding decisions on their behalf. He confided that their greatest concern was that the Sydney branch had heard nothing about the paintings since their theft. They feared that the paintings were already on a ship to obscurity in a European collection as the police had prophesied. An early reward had been considered, but the police quashed that avenue immediately, saying that it was too early and would only hinder their investigations with hundreds of false and misleading prank-calls.

Les asked how much the reward would be if, in six months, the paintings were still unrecovered. The answer he heard was that it is always a standard ten percent offered – fifty thousand dollars in this case.

"And is confidentiality assured?" Les shrewdly asked.

"If an informant goes to the police, then certainly not – we lose control of it," the insurance person regrettably stated. "But if the information for the recovery of the art comes direct to us," he confidently said, "we never reveal our source. It would discourage future informants."

"And does the reward hinge on the arrest and conviction of the art thieves?"

"Definitely not," the actuary swore, confirming what Les already knew but needed to hear from the horse's mouth. "If the paintings are recovered undamaged, and that's vital, we'll save a payout of half a million on this."

Les returned to the bistro-bar to meet with the mark a dozen more times, and each time grew closer by salting his friendship with snippets of information about the criminal underworld of Melbourne, until finally the penny dropped and the actuary asked Les if he were a criminal. (The mark had to take the initiative to avoid suspicion of double-dealing.)

Les explained that he was an SP (Starting Price) bookmaker in Newmarket, and North Melbourne where a variety of criminal types gathered in their local pubs to illegally bet on horses with him and gab the day away with each other when not out rorting. Therefore, by sheer coincidence (this is when the sting came) Les told the actuary he had heard a confirmed whisper that two of the stolen paintings from Sydney were up for sale by an unknown spruiker in Kensington. From that seminal moment, the actuary was hooked.

Swept off to the insurance office and sworn to secrecy, with papers formally signed, Les became an operative for that insurance company, with the single objective of chasing down the spruiker with the possibility of brokering a 'reward' for all the stolen paintings. He even got a reasonable stipend to cover his costs and pay for his efforts. Les performed as promised.

Two months later, acting on an 'anonymous' tip from Sydney (with Les acting as the go-between) the Melbourne insurance firm was directed to a stolen car under the Kings Way bridge in South Melbourne. The six missing paintings in pristine condition sat securely wrapped in blankets on the back seat. The police opinion, aired through the television media that evening, stated: "Obviously the thieves had bitten off more than they could chew. Thefts of this kind are never profitable."

Les said he laughed with his mates when he heard that crock of shit.

3
BACCARAT

WHETHER YOU ARE YOUNG OR OLD IS NOT AN ISSUE: WHAT COUNTS IS HOW MUCH HAS BEEN EXPERIENCED DURING THE JOURNEY

- Joe Tog

Other than greyhounds and tightly controlled horse racing, legitimate venues for other forms of gambling did not exist back in the 70s: so illicit gambling dens abounded. Every major city had them and usually they operated with police sanction.

One particular den I used to regularly frequent in Swanson Street (the main arterial road of Melbourne's CBD) opened its door every night at 11:30 sharp and stayed open until 6 the next morning. Accessed by a long flight of stairs guarded by two heavies (one outside the entrance door on the footpath who doubled as a spruiker, and the other at the top of the stairs), and depending on how many punters turned up, baccarat was invariably the preferred game for the first four hours or so until, in the wee hours of the morning a version of two-up, played with three dice in a cage instead of three pennies tossed in the air, was exchanged for the cards.

The baccarat table – the size of a flatbed truck, I kid you not! – stood in the middle of a large room with narrow windows overlooking the footpath. Covered in green felt, the table doubled for both games. A big H in red had been taped on the felt at one end and a similarly H described T at the other. A wide strip of white tape divided the table across the middle to where a large rectangular space was taped out. The operators kept the bank's money and the card-shoe for baccarat in it, but were quick to swap the shoe for the cage when interest in baccarat waned. The H and T on the table were for the placement of bets before the cage was spun: Heads or Tails.

Made from wire mesh and shaped like an hourglass, suspended in a steel frame, the cage tumbled three different coloured dice (red, yellow, and green) guaranteeing a known result each time the cage stopped. Heads and Tails it was called, with three Hs and three Ts on each of the six-sided die, a win for one side of the table or the other every time the cage was spun: (HHH, HHT, HTT, TTT.) A house tax of 5% was levied on *every* win before payout. A sure-fire earner for all concerned except the punters!

Following a late supper in one of the city restaurants, or after the pubs closed at midnight, I enjoyed playing there and spent hundreds of hours gathering in small wins applying a martingale system, betting on the outcome of those three dice until by chance I became a partner in a baccarat scam perpetrated on the den. I met two characters to whom, in general conversation, I innocently revealed vital information, enabling them to take gambling one step further by improving their luck to such a level that it became a sure thing for all of us. The moment I understood their intention I put my betting system and allegiance to the dice aside, transferring immediately to the certainty of the cards.

Historically, a game of baccarat is a contest between two people only; but in a casino the rules are changed to allow multiple punters to play against the house. During the 70s, all of the illegal games I frequented in Melbourne stayed with the older European rule where two punters played against each other, with onlookers permitted to place bets on the outcome of which player they thought would win. All table bets were covered by the house, and side bets amongst the punters were not permitted.

Two cards are dealt face down to each player. Picture cards and 10s are zero, an ace is one, and all other cards are face value. When the total of two cards is double digit, such as $7+9=16$, the value is in the last number, in this case 6. The same as if it were a pair of 7s, when totalled is 14, makes it 4. When the first two cards equal a 9 or an 8 (nine is the highest), those hands are called a 'natural' – and displayed on the table face-up to win outright. When neither player has a natural a third card is called for, and the higher numbered hand ultimately wins. If the card values total 5 – for example eight and seven $(8+7=15)$ – a dilemma then arises: whether or not to draw a card to boost the 5 in an attempt to beat the other unknown hand. To draw a four would be unbeatable $(5+4=9)$, but to draw a six $(5+6=11)$ takes it back to 1. The scam relied on the fact that a five was pivotal: to call for a card . . . or not call? The exact same odds of improving or worsening exist either way. The third card, if called for, when pulled from the shoe was always dealt face up visible to all punters. If both cards in a hand totalled a low number like 3, an unknown third card could still tip it over the top: 3+9=12, back to 2! Drawn hands were replayed.

Unfortunately for the many regular punters who played there, the house rules called for the largest bettor at either end of the table to be the one who picked up and played the cards. Often those players had no mathematical understanding of the odds, so foolishly called for a third card when it was obvious to savvy players that they should sit! It caused lots of grumbling and dispute amongst the punters. That unpredictable human factor constantly interfering with the purity of baccarat odds was why I only bet on the dice. (Years later the rules were changed so that both hands were played by the *house* face up on the table, thereby eliminating the disputes, and perhaps wittingly, the cheat factor too.)

Experienced card users know that decks of cards are officially sealed by the card manufacturer, and consequently a big production was always made of that fact each night when six decks were handed around to punters at the commencement of play to break the seals and shuffle the cards before placement into the long wooden shoe. The only card fully displayed in the shoe was the back of the first card, and that card was slid out and dealt face down one by one to each player. And finally, when a third card became the decider, a lot of deliberation went into whether or not to call for that blind card.

My betting system (explained at the end of this story for those who enjoy a gamble) always followed the last win of an even bet – rarely does probability come up H T H T H T H T. Other dissimilar combinations are far more common such as, H T T H T H H T H, and so forth. But I set that system aside once I learnt the game was going to be rigged! Within a week I was piggybacking my bets on the bets placed by those two on the table. And win they did!

My change to manufactured luck lasted for about a month. Not extraordinary money, but it came to me steady enough to be pleased with the income supplement. Each time the cards were played by one of those who set it up, the other bet big on the outcome: I confidently followed. They were canny players and signalled me when not to follow their bet, 'suffering' a few runs of intentional losses to allay suspicion by the house that something other than a kiss from Lady Luck was at work. At the conclusion of each night's play, three hundred and twelve used cards (six decks, excluding the twelve jokers removed at the start) were theatrically emptied out of the shoe into a big bin at the door for anyone to take, thereby ensuring that cards which might have been secretly marked by a cheat during the game were out of play forever. Thus, the constant requirement of six new decks every night.

How did they do it? It was quite easy to devise, once the rules of the game are clearly understood, but the implementation of it required steady nerves and great risk. If caught by those crooks that ran the game with the full backing of corrupt police in on the take . . . well, we won't go into that!

The key piece of information unwittingly held by me was that I once saw the operator in a store-room at the rear of the building – always kept locked to deny access to any punter who passed by to use the toilet – and he had carelessly left the door ajar. I had seen him standing at an open cupboard with hundreds of decks of Queen Slipper cards stacked on a middle shelf, along with a carton of toilet rolls above them and cleaning gear haphazardly placed on the floor below – proof positive that the cards were stored on the premises, and not brought to the venue each night as mistakenly believed by all.

An exploratory day spent by me in the back lane and adjacent restaurant to suss out if there was a caretaker in the building confirmed that it was unoccupied during daylight hours (who would want to pinch a gigantic baccarat table, some cards and a few toilet rolls) proving that the next part of the scam could safely proceed.

The purchase of a hundred new packs of Queen Slipper cards by the entrepreneurial two quickly became a hundred packs of perfectly *resealed*, tricked-out card decks: each card accurately identified by a tiny ultra-violet dot invisible to a normal-sighted person, but with the right glasses (they told me) as easy to see as a pimple on your nose.

Using my climbing ability, one hundred packs of perfectly good cards from the cupboard, were switched for one hundred doctored decks mixed in with the fifty or so remaining legitimate decks left. From then on I turned up nightly as regular as clockwork to play baccarat, when at least three or four of the dodgy packs were shuffled into the shoe, until the well of plenty eventually ran dry.

After that I stayed away from the Swanston Street baccarat club (just in case, for health reasons) by changing my venue to North Melbourne and becoming a frequenter of Nap's less notorious two-up game. The two scammers travelled over to Perth where they performed a different rip-off, this time by switching sets of loaded dice in and out when playing craps. And then up to Darwin where I lost track of their adventures.

+ + + +

Addendum:

The following system is recommended for imaginary play or a night of fun at the casino. Do not commit serious money, unless you have plenty to throw away.

Probability of numbers is as certain as the Southern Cross points south in the sky. Spinning the cage over and over will eventually result in ten Heads in a row (odds of 1023:1) yet an eleventh spin of the dice has the same one-in-two chance of resulting in another Head. Inanimate dice have no memory, but a superstitious gambler believes the odds can be influenced, and would think 'it has to change' when confidently placing a bet on the result of the next spin being Tails.

The above actually took place at the venue before the card scam when I and a matronly woman, who confided, "I've been following you, love", stood as the only bettors on H waiting for another spin of the cage. The T side of the table had only a handful of bets scattered over it, a few with personal markers so that punters could recognise their money when it came to collect. And guess what? It again came up H! But unfortunately, I had only placed a five dollar note on the table. (The decision-making had been removed by the system I used as well as determining the amount bet.) And when the next spin happened – going for twelve in a row – I was the sole bettor on H, and only three or four were still willing to bet on T. The dice finally changed their random minds and came up T: nevertheless, I had collected on an extraordinary run of ten Heads in a row. (I missed the first H obviously, when I switched to follow the winning side.) Yet if six thousand spins take place – a Ripley's Believe It Or Not – the mathematical likelihood of eleven in a row happening are three.

Five dollars in the 70s had the same buying power as twenty dollars now, so the dollar amounts in my betting system have been adjusted to reflect that. When added together, the numbers 2, 4, 6, and 8, total twenty. Once all those numbers are cancelled the amount won will be twenty dollars, irrespective of how many bets – won or lost – it took to do so. Add the first and last figure together to establish the amount to bet; in this instance, 2+8=10.

Imagine now that you are with me, back in the roaring 70s gambling together in that smoke-filled baccarat den, as we watch the operator give that cage a spin. Assume H comes up. Place your $10 on the H end of the table and wait for the cage to be spun again . . . then slow down and stop. If H wins again, simply strike off the 2 and the 8, leaving 4 and 6 still to be bet (**2** 4 6 **8**). By adding 4 and 6 you again get 10. Bet $10 on H. (Three in a row is a mystical winning number to gamblers.) This time the cage stops and reveals T wager lost. The amount lost is added to the line of numbers: **2** 4 6 **8** 10. Again, add the first and last numbers together (4+10=14) so wager $14 on T (*follow-the-win* is the mantra). Unluckily, it turns up H. Add the lost fourteen dollars to the list: **2** 4 6 **8** 10 14. Numbers 4 and 14 are combined to make an $18 bet on H (follow-the-win). H won. Hurray!

Cross off the 4 and the 14. The remaining two numbers determine the next bet (**2** **4** 6 **8** 10 **14**), hopefully the last. Combined, 6 and 10 equal $16 wagered on H. And H (seeing as I'm controlling the dice) is what rolled up. When **all** the numbers are cancelled, **2 4 6 8 10 14,** a new game begins. Each time that happens, when all the numbers cancel out, twenty dollars extra goes into your pocket!

The puzzling feature about this unusual betting system when applied to even money bets – red or black; high or low; odd or even – is that *two* numbers are crossed off when it wins, but only *one* number is added when it loses. It is 55/45 your way, rather than the 50/50 when playing even money. Leave when you are ahead. Good luck!

+ + + +

4
UNDER CONCRETE

A common type of floor safe

THERE SHOULD NEVER BE REGRETS:
JUST LESSONS LEARNT

An associate of mine, Ken, brought up the subject of floor safes while watching television together in his lounge room and, after bandying the subject around a bit, directly asked, "Have you ever done one on a job?"

I replied circumspectly by answering, "I gave you the door of a floor safe last year, if you remember." I had purchased the second-hand safe using false ID to understand how the combination worked and to discover if the lift-out circular door could be easily penetrated. Being twelve centimetres thick, and its diameter the same as a DVD, I quickly learned that its strength lay in its compact size: and even if the door could be drilled all the way through to introduce water and an explosive into the cavity of the safe, the energy generated in the explosion would be expended downwards destroying the thin metal box underneath the floor slab and therefore not breach the door. I reminded Ken by saying, "I eventually opened the one I gave you using a scope and pick through a hole I drilled."

"Yeah, I know; you told me that back then. But that's not what I asked." He saw through my attempt to avoid answering his question.

"Not directly, I haven't opened one," I responded honestly, unsure of where this was going. "But I was in on a bungled attempt back in the 70s to blow one in a TAB. It had a sliding door, on rails fixed in the concrete floor. We were lucky to have got away; the cops and security were so quick to respond."

"What about a smaller floor-safe," he queried. "With a bigger door than the one you gave me?" I knew that a job was in the air by the way he probed, if it could be done. My answer was by way of an explanation.

"If it's a better model than the door I gave you, then I don't know how to do it. To drill eight centimetres like I did with the other one to get a scope through the alloy and into the back of the combination took me three hours." I gave it some more thought while the television droned on in the background before adding, "And that's without the worry of noise on the job."

"But it could be done?" he queried.

I asked, "What kind of place is it?"

"A house," he said. "It's in Balwyn." Ken raised his eyebrows indicating significance, as if I should recognise the cue.

I guessed, "Is this the dude you've been telling me about?"

Ken just nodded. Apparently, according to strong rumour, this guy's company was under investigation by the Australian Tax Office. He had swindled hundreds of thousands of dollars out of local councils over non-existent office materials, as well as defrauding large personal investments made with him by some trusting individuals. I suspected Ken might have been one of the latter, though he never admitted it to me.

"So you actually have his address now," I stated, knowing that to be fact.

Again, he simply nodded.

I immediately asked, "Do you know if it's a new house, or an old one?", as an idea I had been developing for some time sprang instantly to mind.

"Fifteen years," he answered, hazarding a guess at its age, indicating to me that he had already been there and sussed the place out. In the leafy streetscapes of Balwyn, that meant a relatively new house.

"And what did it look like to you?" (Meaning, was it doable?)

"Split level, two-storied, with a swimming pool down the back, and a double garage at the front. And two alarms, hooked into those friggin' sensor-lights everywhere."

Ken had certainly done his homework. Back-to-back alarms were unusual and generally indicated a level of paranoia – or hidden wealth – with sensors and a camera linked, well-concealed and rigged to dial a phone number direct. Sufficient proof to me that more than just general house contents were being protected; and I'm sure Ken thought the same. I told him I was interested.

"I'm contacting a guy in Sydney about the alarm, but he hasn't got back to me yet." That meant a stranger from another crew, an introduction I didn't like. I quickly voiced my opposition.

"Sorry, I'm not doing it with someone else. I thought it was just us and ---"

He cut me off, saying, "Only for info, Joe. The first box I know how to disable; it's in the garage and is the original one from when the house was built. But there's a pad at the bottom of the stairs in the lounge room, a new type I've never seen before, and so I took a few pics to get an ID of it."

I then asked him the most important question for my plan to work. "Do you know where the safe is?" My idea for outwitting the strength of its door would also circumvent the alarm system, provided it was a floor safe.

"I'd say it's downstairs because the second alarm only protects that area," he confidently stated. "But as for being sure, I don't know."

"And where's the main bedroom?" I inquired.

"Upstairs," he confidently stated. "But I know him and his missus sleep in the bedrooms below."

"How many bedrooms are there?"

"Four: two upstairs and another two off the lounge below which overlooks the pool."

"How can you be certain they don't use the bedrooms above?"

"I'm not a hundred percent sure. But I've been there twice when the television went off, and no lights came on upstairs."

That sounded good enough for me. What he said made sense, but nevertheless I shy away from too much speculation. "How do you know it's a floor safe?"

"I figure it must be, by what he once said when I took my sales-book to him to get tax advice." Finally, proof now that this was more personal than he was letting on.

"And I'm sure you're going to enlighten me?" I prompted, interested in his reasoning.

"He told me I'd be better off sticking my extra cash under the dresser, to avoid GST bullshit." Ken looked at me to see if I understood the point he was making. I had no idea what he was alluding to, and said so.

Ken elaborated, a bit peeved by my show of ignorance. "It's not like he said 'stick it under a mattress' or 'put it in a draw'; you know what I mean?" Ken spread his hands, as he added, "I reckon it's one of those Freud things – where he stashes his black – under the dresser in a floor safe! I reckon he's had one put in."

It was so basic that the Freudian slip Ken alluded to rang true for me too. And even if his reasoning was cockeyed, it nevertheless would still boil down to the likelihood of something of considerable value kept in his bedroom. Why else pay for a second alarm, a bit like wearing a belt with braces, when presumably, one should be sufficient? Firstly, though, I wanted to find out if my floor safe theory could be applied, before a direct assault was needed to gain entry.

"When do I get to see the place?" I asked, my mind racing ahead envisaging actions not yet carried out.

+ + + +

The night was cold, and a drizzle of rain had started with thick clouds above: perfect weather for scouting around. Wearing a fisherman's cap and my denim jacket zipped, I scurried down the dark sideway of a large house, following Ken as he scrambled over a locked gate. Inside the backyard where a side fence would normally have been, we crouched concealed in bushes on a rocky embankment to peer down into the neighbouring property. Moonlight filtering through the clouds revealed a swimming pool with slate paths glistening wet below us, a gated entrance in deep misty shadow higher up, with concrete steps and tiered garden beds everywhere. The upper level of the house we were interested in sat bathed in streetlight; but the lawn visible below the retaining wall of the pool sloped down to the far corner of the property and lay in deep shadow. As I expected it to be, everything was exactly as Ken had described.

The side of the house facing us had a patio with concrete furniture where the lounge room windows were dimly lit and, because of our slight elevation, I could see over the top of the curtain pelmets into the room. I couldn't hear a television from where I hid, but the variation in light flickering above the thick curtains made it obvious that one was on. Except for the usual night sounds of suburbia with a dog barking in the distance, the place was as tranquil as a graveyard, but not as innocuous: security lights lurked everywhere, even the yard we were in. Ken nudged me and gave a flick of his head, indicating that I should follow him.

Having a dog wandering about in the back yard is, without a doubt, the best early warning system to a householder; but the next best deterrent against burglars is a highly visible, inaccessible outdoor camera: one that records movement whether or not the security lighting is triggered. That implies to the would-be thief that other less-visible cameras might also exist inside, but Ken had assured me that neither were installed at this place. And I trusted his surveillance skills; otherwise I would not have been there risking my freedom.

Ken took off and I stepped in his footsteps, following his confident descent down the rocky slope towards the outer wall of the swimming pool. In a running crouch he circled the retaining wall of the pool headed for the other side of the property, while I ran behind him, worried over where a sensor would eventually be encountered and light us up like rabbits caught in a spotlight beam. But within a few minutes we were safely huddled next to the house wall, behind a lemon tree in deep cover, undetected.

"That window there," Ken explained with a slight pant to his speech, pointing to a small opaque one above his head, "is the toilet for the living room. I've heard them use it. And further along are the bedrooms with a bathroom suite in between." Peering up the wall towards where he gestured, I could just make out the casement of the first bedroom window with the rest of the wall lost from sight in wild plant growth and darkness. A metre-wide series of ascending steps, dripping water in the moonlight, rose in stages between the house and the side fence towards a door in the rear wall of the garage at street level. The entire area was overgrown with bushes and shrubs that had been left unattended for years: a perfect haven for anyone to watch from. In whispered conversation we mooted a few ideas around.

"We could just go in and grab 'em," Ken proposed. "Make the bastards give it up." But I knew that was said to get our brain cells working. Violence attracts publicity and police heat and is always, *always* counterproductive.

Ignoring what he said, I asked, "How are you going to deal with the alarms?" They were his area of expertise, so it was up to him to have a solution.

"Love you, long time," he said, alluding to a method commonly used by those with patience and skill. It involved tactics spread over weeks, to gain entry in slow increments, such as disabling a reed-switch on an entrance door or a window often left unlocked or even open when the building is occupied and the alarm is off. A small screwdriver, with lots of dash and stealth exercised, will remove the cover and expose the two contacts inside the switch buried in the frame, directly above the magnet in the door or window which opens and closes the electrical contact. A tiny twist of silver-paper pressed in tight will bridge the circuit permanently. Or a riskier way to neutralise the switch, when the alarm is active, is to carefully drill through the frame to gain access. A similar method can be applied by drilling through the mortise plate on the door frame. A bit of putty and paint judiciously applied will conceal it from all but the expert eye until a stiff piece of wire is inserted to force back the lock – and entry is gained.

When an internal sensor detects movement within a building the alarm is instantly triggered sending a warning down the phone-line, and simultaneously sets the sirens clamouring; and while that is happening, Ken would be rushing around moving a sensor or two out of alignment so that his *next* entry would go undetected. Security and/or police responding to the alarm *should* log it as a false alarm when making their report because no forced entry would be apparent; or blame the starling seen flying around inside released by Ken on his way out before locking the door behind him. If the interference of the internal sensors is overlooked . . . then Bob's your uncle!

After considered thought, I finally proposed my idea to Ken, saying, "While you're doing that – because it *might* be an upright safe, and maybe not even in the bedroom – I want to go in under the slab."

Ken stared at me, a look of puzzlement on his feature. "You what?" he asked.

"Under the slab: I'm sure it can be done to find a floor safe."

"What are you talking about?" he queried, unable to grasp the concept.

"Right now the concrete slab for both bedrooms is above us, it's just that we're outside the building, but if…"

"It's built on solid rock, mate!" he sniggered at my apparent ignorance, kicking the wet rockery near his feet for emphasis. "No fucking way!"

"Being this rocky is a problem for a builder," I told him. "I've dug footings for a factory – you haven't – and I know when rock is excavated, plenty of sand is used to backfill, and most times the formwork for the foundations is temporary and jerry-built."

Builders commonly employ excessive use of sand to level the

ground, before laying thick plastic over it when preparing for a concrete slab. And particularly like this building where the floor is split into two levels on a slope with lots of rocks, water pipes and sewerage involved, the in-ground footings which support the slab become very complicated.

"I need to know if foam has been substituted anywhere instead of wood." The look of doubt from Ken compelled me to explain more: "Styrofoam is used because it's easier than wood to cut into odd shapes and I can't know if it's been used until I've taken a look under the house."

Ken stared at me, not saying a word in response to what I'd just stated. I felt I had to say more, thinking that he thought my marbles were lost. "At least it's worth a look – a steel box is all a floor-safe consists of under a slab of concrete, with ten or twelve centimetres of ready-mix poured around the collar and down the sides – that's no defence against us. And if it doesn't work out," I finished off, "we still have your way. What do you think?"

He shook his head back and forth, not uttering a word . . . then suddenly, he was up and off, with me responding as though a dog was at our heels. I had no idea why he had run, but I reacted instinctively by following him.

At the far side of the swimming pool, Ken stopped as suddenly as he had started, dropping to his knees next to the low wall. Kneeling in the wet grass beside him, our eyes were level with the slate path circling the pool. He extended his hand through the pool fence, pointing across the dark water at a shadowed area in a slate wall below one of the very large floor-to-ceiling living room windows. Ken whispered, "That's where the chemicals for the pool are kept."

An entry point! I should already have known there had to be one to allow access for maintenance. I made a move to get closer, but he restrained me by placing his hand on my shoulder, whispering, "Twin lights cover the pool this end, and I haven't moved 'em." He pointed.

Studying the roofline, I could just see them beneath the guttering, pointing forty-five degrees away from each other, ready to illuminate the water and path if their sensor detected movement. I lay there frustrated, trying to think of a simple way to outwit the lights as...

"Hang on!" I suddenly exclaimed. "How do you know what's kept in there?"

"I watched the pool-guy get his chemicals out," he casually replied. And as an afterthought, added, "It's not locked, you know."

Of course, I should have realised: go in under the house and inspect it during daylight hours. It didn't matter if the lights came on then! I curbed my urge to know more until another time; enough had been learned to satisfy me that my proposal was feasible. I hinted to Ken that we should not push our luck. We left there, as unremarked as we had entered, agreeing to revisit and convert the next part of our venture into action.

The following morning at nine o'clock, Ken and I sat in his utility parked a few houses down the street from our target. We had earlier walked together and confirmed that one car sat in the garage, but when leaving the night before we saw there had been two. Ken confidently stated that the remaining vehicle belonged to the target's wife. Watching through the rear window of the ute, we waited for her to leave so that one of us could scout under the house. Unfortunately it had to be me; Ken never had a clue of what to look for.

The roller door suddenly lifted and, as I nudged Ken to take notice, the car we had been hoping to see emerged and stopped at the roadside gutter. The roller descended slowly to again fit flush with the concrete driveway. Not till then did the car head up the street and disappear in the direction of the shops on the main road.

Expecting the car to soon return, I left Ken to keep nit and walked with a purpose towards the entry gate between the house and the fence separating the house next door. The large bushes and verdant growth at the front concealed me nicely from neighbours as I clambered over the gate to drop down onto the concrete path inside. I sped down the steps straight to the rear of the house and headed for the small maintenance door Ken had pointed out to me the night before. It was made of metal and had a sturdy pad-bolt fitted, but no lock hung on the door to secure it. The security lights that had come on didn't bother me. Cautiously, I eased it open . . . not knowing what to expect . . . and certainly not the spaciousness and metal shelving revealed inside. With the door pulled closed behind me, torch-beam questing about behind the shelves, what I saw confirmed exactly what I wanted to see.

5
TWINE

Australian bank notes

FAILURE IS INSTRUCTIVE

If you have never heard of the Twine and object to the thought of a stranger stealing your money – then read on. And if you *have* heard of it, or even been a victim of it, and would like to understand the mechanics of how the Twine is done, then this story will reveal all.

+ + + +

Brian spoke quietly and dressed conservatively like an office worker or public servant. He always showed good manners and courteous behaviour. I watched him one afternoon scam a few shopkeepers in Johnson Street, Fitzroy, and come away at the end of it laughing while splitting the 'take' with me.

A few times I tried copying Brian but failed miserably. Not because I couldn't master the Twine, but because it didn't feel right in the doing. Similar to passing a dud cheque – which I have never done – because I know that type of fleecing is not for me.

The New Zealand media lambasted Brian as being an Australian conman capable of taking money by fraudulent tactics, and after being arrested and serving a short stretch in Auckland Prison on a deception charge, he was deported back to Australia with *persona non gratia* stamped on his passport, never able to return. But Brian was unbothered by that ban; he often bad-mouthed the legal system in the land of the Long White Cloud as being prejudiced towards Australians.

Wherever money changes hands in exchange for goods the Twine can and will be applied but, by understanding how it is conducted, its 'bite' is avoidable. A number of ways have been devised by retail businesses to prevent the abuse and is used effectively by trained staff. But over time people forget, or they get replaced, so the scam is constantly reborn. Anyway, this is one version of how the Twine is done.

✦ ✦ ✦ ✦

Cruising along the mall, Brian comes to a shop open for business. Casual-like, he stops and looks into the display window, but not to view the goods – he needs to know how many staff are inside. One is ideal, Brian told me; even two is all right; but he advises three or more should be given a miss.

There are two staff standing together, an old guy with a young female assistant. Brian checks his working cash: a $50 note in the right-hand pocket, a $5 note in the left-hand pocket, with $3 worth of small change in his back pocket. He strolls through the doorway and stops at the counter.

"Good afternoon. Beautiful day, isn't it," Brian cheerfully greets them both: then targets the one in charge. "I'd like a kilo of bacon, please."

The shop guy smiles and responds by saying, "Certainly. What type?"

"Any kind will do," Brian answers. "How much is it?" he asks.

"Roebucks' is best at just over five dollars a kilogram. Would you like that?"

"Sure thing," Brian says, "that'll do," affecting a casual attitude while gazing about the shop's interior to see what the woman is doing. Brian explained that other staff usually went about their business and did not watch.

"Here you are," said the smiling storekeeper as he places the bacon on the counter in front of Brian. "That will be five-dollars-thirty. Is there anything else?"

"Ah…thank you," Brian stumbles along, faking it. "No, there isn't anything else." Brian acts as though he is distracted by what the assistant is doing, pulling out the coins first, and pretending to watch the woman jiggle as she tidies the counter top. (Every little bit helps to convince the mark that he is vague or stupid.)

Brian deposits the thirty cents from his back pocket on the counter. The $50 note quickly follows, taken from his right pocket without looking, placing it beside the 'smash' already on the counter. Throughout all of that, Brian kept watching the female assistant.

The smiling shopkeeper picks up the $50 note, and then the coins. The timing for Brian is now crucial; otherwise it will fail no matter what he does. With the bacon package in hand, transaction completed, Brian walks casually towards the door as though to leave. The shopkeeper now has two choices: to call Brian back for his 'forgotten' change, or let him continue on out the door.

"Excuse me!" the shopkeeper calls out. "You've forgotten your change," extending the money towards Brian, a look of superiority on his face.

Brian hurries back. "Did I give you a fifty?" he queries. "I thought I handed you a five!" Adding as an afterthought when he reached the counter, "My mind must have wandered." Forty-five dollars is counted into Brian's hand: a $20 note, two $10 notes, and a $5 note.

Showing a bit of indecision now, Brian says, "I have a five-dollar note in my pocket somewhere. Please exchange a ten-dollar note for the two fives." Without waiting for acknowledgment he separates the five from the money in his hand, and then checks his pockets, acting confident, presuming the shopkeeper will agree.

With his head down, Brian sneaks a look to make certain the shopkeeper extracts a $10 note from the till *before* he gets to take hold of Brian's two fives. And while the shopkeeper is distracted at the drawer (without him or the assistant seeing) Brian palms one of the two $10 notes (from the change of the $50 note) and slips it into his back pocket. He continues to rummage in his pockets for the $5 note, and again checks on the woman.

The moment the shopkeeper produces the $10 note from the till, Brian says to him, "Here's the five!" pulling it from his left pocket, holding it up. "I knew I had one on me." He slaps the $5 note on top of the money held in his other hand. The shopkeeper of course subconsciously thinks – or should if he has been played right –there is now a total of fifty dollars held in Brian's hand: $45 in change originally handed by him to Brian, plus the $5 note he just watched Brian add.

Brian needs to grab hold of that $10 note first, before handing over his two $5 notes in exchange. If the shopkeeper takes Brian's money first, it may not work.

Brian babbled bullshit at this point for continuity as he reached for the ten. He knew the maxim *the customer is always right* would be adhered to by the obliging shopkeeper. As Brian knows, the shopkeeper has undoubtedly dealt with hundreds of duds just like him.

Grasping in his palm the $10 note just handed to him, Brian fumbles both $5 notes into the shopkeeper's waiting hand, counting each note as it falls: "five . . . and five . . . is ten." (Brian still holds a total of thirty dollars in one hand: a $20 and a $10, PLUS the $10 note just exchanged, scrunched in his other hand.) "Sorry about that," he meekly says, and continues to talk. *The timing of the next step is all-important to successfully gull the shopkeeper.* If timed too early, he will twig to the attempted con: and if acted-out too late, it simply will not work.

As the second $5 note goes into the till — by now the shopkeeper's mind should have shifted from the $10 exchange — Brian's friendly demeanour abruptly changes, to a display of bad temper. He aggressively states, "I want my fifty-dollar note back!"

He thrusts his money-filled hand across the countertop towards the till and dumps the cash (a $20 and two $10 notes) and menacingly demands, "Take this! Give me back my fifty-dollar note!" Brian's hands are displayed empty, palms shown for all to see, imperiously beckoning with his fingers for the fifty. Into the till in quick succession (following the two $5 notes) go a $20 note, and two $10 notes in all, a total of fifty dollars!

By this time the shopkeeper *should* be well and truly bamboozled by the money-shuffle and glad to be rid of him. Brian cheerfully accepts the $50 note handed to him across the counter and quickly retreats with his kilo of bacon.

For all that bafflement, Brian gained an extra ten bucks; the

$10 note he earlier slipped surreptitiously into his back pocket!
He paid for the bacon.

+ + + +

6
TROJAN HORSE

Circa 1960 Chubb combination safe

A TRUE FRIEND IS ANOTHER SELF

"If you don't mind telling me, just for old time sake, I'd like to know how you guys pulled it off." The sergeant of police looked at me earnestly.

"You've got it wrong; we didn't do it."

"But we suspected it was you; and police intelligence later confirmed that it *was* the Pub gang. I led the team that responded to the callout and…"

"It wasn't us," I interjected. "The jacks in Adelaide were running their own agenda and accused us of every crime in the region at that time." The old sergeant stared at me, close to retirement, and this mystery must have played on his mind for a long time; he tried one more question, but posed it as a statement. "I've never been able to work out how a place could be broken into, a safe blown, and then get away in in six minutes. That's how long it took us to race there from the station once the alarms triggered." He went on to add, "We had three premises as possibilities your gang might hit, and that safe job was one of them." He gazed at me, expectant, believing his frankness would pay.

I had no intention of confirming anything, even though the offence occurred years prior to this conversation; *tell them nothing* was my policy then, and it still is now when it comes to current stuff I know about. We were conversing in a hallway of the Horsham Courthouse waiting for my hearing to commence. Extradition proceedings against me had been ongoing for eighteen months in Adelaide, South Australia, until now – Commonwealth Law had finally overruled State Law – I waited for the Victorian court to take me into custody to serve out an unexpired parole period fourteen years old!

I owed the Victorian Parole Board ten months of a twelve month parole which I refused to serve in Victoria. I moved interstate without their consent and washed my hands of them. They took it personally, and pursued me like a blood vendetta until finally I was forced to agree to a deal through the Adelaide courts to surrender myself at Horsham. This was the culmination of that deal.

"You couldn't be charged now even if we wanted to," he proclaimed. "It was so long ago."

I again reiterated, "We didn't do it." My mind was made up. Our talk skirted around the subject of crime a bit more and it was about then I heard my name called to enter the courtroom. We never met again after that.

That same afternoon, two uniformed constables transported me in an unmarked police car to the Remand Centre at Pentridge.

After a thorough search I was handed a meal and then locked in a cell, with nothing to read, no television and no radio. The conversation with the old sergeant at Horsham had dredged up a bucket load of memories, now that my mind settled on the past to entertain me, until sleep overtook my thoughts. This is how it went down.

+ + + +

"I will drill the safe and overcharge it," Fritz announced in his precise English. "Enough to blow the door off – it can't do much damage in that place." I agreed with him but had to say more.

"Have you got a place to stand out of the blast area?" I asked. "That's taking a big risk." Fritz had tried that dangerous method once before on another job in the hinterland of New South Wales and ended up seriously injured.

"A concrete pillar holds up the roof right near it. I will be fine." He had more dash than Arthur Delaney (a notorious jewel thief), but when it came to explosives I worried for him.

"You can't do it in that time," I exclaimed, concerned, having given it heavy thought. "Four minutes isn't long enough."

We had driven a direct course from the nearest twenty-four hour police station to the job back and forth three times, knowing that the alarm dialled direct to them once the second alarm tripped. Each drive had taken us just under five minutes. I saw no way of bettering the time factor without the possibility of police becoming suspicious.

Alarm sensors which detected internal movement were not practical in the way this business operated. Birds constantly got in past the roller doors, mice roamed the building, and suspended signs swayed in the slightest air movement when the weather outside picked up. Therefore, to make up for the compromise on security, the building had *two* perimeter alarm systems installed: unusual, but smart. The original alarm, fitted to guard the roof and all possible entry points after the building's completion, relied on audible bells and flashing lights to warn the public or a roving watchman of a forced entry. An untalented thief could easily disarm it with expander-foam and side-cutters. But the second more comprehensive system, fitted years later when the business picked up, was sophisticated; silent, and cross-wired in such a way that certainty of detection existed if tampered with. It relied on passive infra-red to register movement, and then activated a dialler to dispatch its warning down a secure phone-line. While an unwary thief believed he had the run of the place, police were speeding to his downfall. As a consequence, because of the silent alarm and the certainty of a quick police response, the safe was not as good as it should have been, considering the amount of cash it held after the pre-Christmas weekend sales.

Fritz had come up with a daring way to circumvent the elaborate alarm and an undetected entry carried out by him three days earlier satisfied both of us that re-entry in the same way and unrestricted access to the safe was a shoe-in. Fritz had taken three close-up Polaroids of the safe-door for minute study with me later, to ensure agreement on how to defeat it as well as rehearse each stage and the time required.

The rear wall of the building backed on to a creek-cum–drain overhung with willow trees, infested with weeds and rubbish of every kind; the building therefore lacked a back entrance. But it did have a long row of windows with padlocked metal grills on the outside covering each one. The window frames were fitted with reed-switches to detect forced entry and the glass had metallic alarm-tape on the inside in the event of it being smashed. This would be the exit point for Fritz.

During cold or wet nights I have learnt that most people sleep soundly and by about two-thirty to three o'clock, everyone is in bed dreaming. And that coincides with the time police are halfway through their shift and thinking about a cup of coffee and a pit-stop back at the station. The weather bureau had predicted a cold night for the night we did it, so we figured the early hours of morning was the optimum time to blow the safe. I dropped Fritz off near the place an hour before lock-up: about 4 pm. Our plans were set for 3 am, Monday.

+ + + +

Wearing a blue track-suit and shouldering a lumpy rucksack, Fritz brazenly entered the Staff Only area carrying a cardboard box addressed to that building in large capital letters with official-looking papers attached to a clip-board sitting on top.

He walked confidently towards the inner sanctum office area, separate from the public, homing in on a stack of pallets holding freight, piled high abut the office. A few storehouse workers saw him, but as expected they paid no attention to a courier delivering a package.

The moment Fritz felt unobserved and near enough to do so he slipped behind the pallets and waited . . . watching where he entered to learn if he had been seen and followed. Five minutes of vigilant waiting reassured him that the next step could be taken. He slid the clipboard under a pallet to get rid of it, and then carefully concealed the box for later retrieval: it held two pry-bars, a long electrical lead, a large power drill, ear-muffs, screwdriver and twenty 12 mm masonry drill-bits with extra-long shanks. Not quite all the ingredients needed to break into a safe. The remaining requirements were in his rucksack: gelignite, detonators, wire and batteries, as well as an assortment of special drill-bits.

Fritz carefully scaled the wooden pallets and stealthily gained access on to the false ceiling above the office area. Satisfied that he was concealed from sight he relaxed between ceiling joists, removing the rucksack to use as a pillow to make it comfortable while waiting for the building to be locked down tight. No alarms could reach him there.

The light inside slowly faded after the staff departed . . . the building became tomb-like, dark enough inside to satisfy Fritz that it was time to move. He descended with the rucksack to his box and carried it directly to the entry door into the office network, careful not to deviate outside the boundary set by his earlier undetected incursion.

He slipped the simple lock using a plastic card, and once inside snibbed the door-lock behind him. Everything needed to carry out the job was now in the office section with him, leaving no reason to exit until just before the explosion. Fritz removed his walkie-talkie: it was time to make contact.

+ + + +

The police station swarmed with usual activity, not yet scaled down for the night-shift, so I returned to the creek area behind the building to get within range of Fritz's two-way and tell him not to make a move yet.

"The guys are still out fishing," I told Fritz. (Meaning police were active.) *"So don't get the barbie going just yet."* If an alarm clamoured now there would be an overwhelming response to the break-in, and not the one or two vehicles we expected when things went off the rails near three o'clock. I knew Fritz would boil the jug in the staff lunch room, and settle back in an office chair to wait my call while enjoying a cuppa.

Two hours later, at 8 pm., concealed in bushes at the rear of the building, I again made contact with Fritz. *"The guys are heading back."* (The night-shift police had returned from their first patrol.) *"I'm ready to go, too."*

Fritz confirmed his understanding by transmitting, *"I'll put a few shrimps on the barbie."* He knew I now stood picket outside the building, determined to warn and prepared to assist him in the event of police arriving unexpectedly.

In moonlight and shifting shadows as clouds moved across the sky, concealed by overhanging tree branches, I sawed with a hacksaw a rusty padlock which secured a hinged grill covering one of the rear windows.

+ + + +

Inside, Fritz finalised his preparations to drill the safe. The office desk and filing cabinets had been shunted to the walls to clear the carpet in front of the large safe, and the power lead plugged into a wall socket and attached to the drill. A variety of containers gathered from the lunchroom, now filled with water, lined one side of the safe, while a small desk lamp cast a bright beam of light onto the steel door.

To simply charge the lock-boxes with explosives via the keyholes and hope for the best when detonated demonstrated lack of experience and guaranteed failure. Admittedly this safe was an outdated one, built for an earlier era, but nevertheless its design was capable of resisting the explosive power of gelignite if the conventional safe-breaking method of attacking the locks was applied. High-speed tantalum drills were not available to the public in the 50s when this safe was manufactured – but they became available a decade later, and Fritz had ten of them in his bag.

The front door of the safe consisted of a twenty millimetre plate of case-hardened drill-resistant steel, backed by a sheet of copper to counter gas-cutting. A seventy-five millimetre cavity, spanning the entire inside of the door, contained the many locking bars and two lock-boxes. A further two hundred millimetre metal box, filled with asbestos and concrete to protect the contents from fire, made up the remainder of the door, designed to split apart when an explosive fired in the cavity or a lock-box.

The cavity absorbed the initial expansion of gas as retaining bolts in the door resisted momentarily before they were snapped in two; the front section bulged out, or blew off if overcharged, while the inside half was driven inwards like a plug of compacted steel, so tight that it would require a second charge to remove it. A very dangerous task to do in such a volatile situation and it usually ended up perforating the money so badly that even a rookie constable would know by its distinctive smell and condition how you came by it.

Modern explosives have indestructible microscopic bar-coded balls for tracing history, but it is not them that does the damage to the money; gelignite burns, and it's all those millions of tiny fire-balls developing energy at a rate beyond human comprehension that expands from a solid into a gas in a micro-second resulting in such destruction.

To circumvent all of that, Fritz would laboriously drill through the door, to gain access to the shelves where the prize sat, then drown everything in water to protect it before introducing the gelignite inside so that the explosive force would blast the entire door outwards. Every aspect of a safe is designed to thwart and prevent unlawful entry, not exit! Houdini miraculously escaped from many locked safes, even underwater, because of that knowledge.

Fritz had already removed the handle, exposing the square stub of the thick shaft that operated a cog inside to open the door. Made of cast-iron and designed to fracture if force is foolishly used to twist the handle, Fritz set about doing just that. With the walkie-talkie ear-plug inserted, he hammered the stub to smithereens knowing that outside, someone stood sentinel as his ears and eyes listening and watching for him.

With the stub broken off and the rest of its shaft inside levered out of the way with a screwdriver, the first hundred millimetres of so-called impenetrable safe door had been easily conquered. After fitting a bit in the drill, Fritz inserted it through the hole into the cavity and commenced boring into the metal wall on which all the locking mechanism hung and both lock-boxes were screwed to.

+ + + +

No sound penetrated to the outside where I kept nit across the street behind a high cyclone-wire fence in an unlit council yard. The padlock had been successfully cut from the window grill at the rear of the building and thrown in the creek, with another lock looking as equally weathered hanging unlocked in its place. At my feet lay an old sledgehammer head with a new handle fitted ready to go into action, to smash down the front door seconds after Fritz blew the safe, misdirecting pursuers into believing the perps entered and, most importantly, exited via that front door. If everything went to plan, Fritz would be clambering out the back window at about the same time the police arrived.

The nit-keeping dragged as midnight crawled by and the morning hours grew colder. I was constantly alert to every set of headlights, twice making urgent contact with Fritz to warn of a nightwatchman on patrol checking premises in that street, and again when a divvy van cruised silently like a hunter through the area.

+ + + +

Fritz was in a sweat; he had two tantalum drill-bits left and had not yet pierced the back plate into the body of the safe. The concrete and asbestos mix with thousands of metal pieces included had completely destroyed his twenty masonry bits. He figured only a centimetre or so of drilling remained. A steel-cutting bit will penetrate masonry, but only for a few millimetres, and then after that it becomes useless. He reluctantly fitted one of his remaining two steel-cutting bits. The inside plate still had to be penetrated.

The drill smelt electrical and was smoking; it could easily burn out. He kept alert not to apply too much pressure . . . and after two minutes of steady drilling he stopped to rest the drill and allow it to cool down. The end of the bit felt blunt when he withdrew it to study, and it was super hot. He fitted his last bit.

Sliding it back in the hole he noted that less than twenty millimetres remained visible between the steel door and the chuck of the drill. Forgetting how close to failure it was, he gave the drill full power and drove it aggressively in and out like a hammer-drill, frustrated, now that he knew it could barely cut. It broke through the final sheet of metal! By a stroke of luck he had fitted a tantalum bit exactly when it had been needed.

Fritz could work tirelessly when a special effort was called for, but the arduous drilling had physically challenged him: three hours in the same crouched position, the constant noise of the drill blanketing all other sound except for the ear-bud. With the most dangerous aspect of the caper still to be carried out, Fritz lay on the carpet to rest awhile, to review his next step.

+ + + +

At 2.20 am. I activated the beeper on my two-way to alert Fritz. He needed to get an update every twenty minutes as it approached go-time, and I felt a nervous tension rising within me as the time grew nearer. I could only guess at how Fritz must be feeling.

+ + + +

Fritz awoke, startled by the beeping ear-bud. He had fallen asleep! He quickly thumbed the talk button to learn if things were still on track.

The day previously, in the comfort of his own home, Fritz stuffed three 60 cm lengths of 10 mm plastic tube with gelignite. At one end of each tube a space had been left to accommodate an electric detonator; the other end he stoppered with a waterproof sealant. Altogether, a whole stick of gelignite had been used to fill the tubes; better too much than too little when overcharging, he had decided.

Fritz grabbed his rucksack and pulled out an assortment of articles:

a large funnel with a length of the same 10 mm tubing used to hold the gelignite taped to its end, three rolls of extra-wide gaffer tape, a spool of fishing line, and a wooden pencil case swathed in bubble-wrap with a large coil of fine insulated wire taped on top. He spent twenty minutes applying the tape to seal the door of the safe, making it watertight except for the top section to allow the escape of air when water went in. Satisfied, he inserted the funnel-tube into the drilled hole and taped it to the door. His two-way beeped at 2.40 am.

Fritz sat on the carpet and for the first time brought the detonators into dangerous proximity of the gelignite. Opening the pencil case he exposed to view three slim golden detonators (not the fatter silver type commonly used by quarrymen) each with two wires attached: one blue and the other white, rolled in a small coil.

Unwinding the wires he carefully pushed the detonator into the end of the first tube until it was fully inserted. He repeated the same process with the other two gelignite-filled tubes. After a thick application of quick-drying glue to each detonator to prevent water shorting out their wires, Fritz grabbed the spool of fishing line and tied long lengths midway to each tube. When completely satisfied with his handiwork, he carefully placed the tubes of explosives beside the safe. Next, he poured the containers of water into the funnel, hurrying off to refill them many times until the funnel refused to empty, spewing water back out through the hole. The safe was now half full of water as intended, to protect whatever was immersed inside from being burnt.

In total concentration, Fritz gradually pushed a tube through the hole into the bowels of the safe. If a detonator were crushed now, Fritz would be no more. And he knew it. Slowly, he repeated the dangerous process two more times. By pulling the three fishing lines back towards himself and tying them off, ultra-careful not to tug any of the six detonator wires by mistake, he gently eased the three tubes of explosives together, intertwining them so that even in the worst scenario, if two detonators failed to fire, the remaining detonator would initiate all three tubes.

+ + + +

At 3.00 am, I called Fritz and learned that he wasn't ready yet. *"I'm going for a walk,"* I advised. Being so close to such an outcome made me tense just thinking about it; my bowels rumbled nervously.

Mist shrouded the creek as it grew even colder, contrary to how warm I felt jogging my way back to the hole in the council yard fence. I had carried out a quick scout of the area; strung fishing line strategically between trees and fences to discourage pursuit from upstream; then returned to the sledgehammer to get set for my role in the pending action soon to unfold, knowing that when it did an almighty bang would shake the building and send a tremor through its foundations.

Standing behind a vehicle in the dark yard, after listening to the police scanner for the last time, I made a final call to confirm with Fritz that all was go. *"Give me five minutes,"* Fritz stated. *"And then it will be done."* I gave two beeps back to confirm acknowledgement.

Pocketing the scanner, I held the two-way ready to receive Fritz's last call, knowing only an emergency now would require me to use it. With the sledge in hand I moved out into the moonlight, my mind totally focused, prepared to do whatever it took. But I worried; the watchman was long overdue for his third patrol.

+ + + +

Inside the building, Fritz had just completed the penultimate step. The reel of fine electrical wire had been joined to the six detonator wires hanging out the hole in the safe and unwound through the office and out the door to the concrete roof support behind which he now stood ready to touch to the terminals of a D-cell battery he held. Every piece of possible evidence used by Fritz during the crime, including the drill, had been gathered together and deposited as junk inside a wall cavity of the office. Fritz made his last call.

BAROOOM! *The explosion sounded exactly like a distant clap of thunder, muted as it was inside the building (if it had happened during a storm the sound would have gone unnoticed) except for the raucous discord of the many alarm bells and sirens it triggered throughout the building! Alarms in two adjacent buildings, triggered by the vibrations, started their sirens wailing in noisy sympathy.*

While I hammered the public entry door off its hinges (when the police entered here they would hopefully get lost in the maze of rooms and miss the staff door which connected to the office and freight area) Fritz raced back into the absolute chaos of the office where the demolished safe door had been blasted across the room. It had smashed the desk into kindling as it passed through a wooden partition into another office, finishing up against a brick wall in a tangled mess of steel plate, concrete, and bars. The body of the safe had reeled about and finished on its side with most of its contents spewed along the way. The plaster ceiling hung in tatters, and the ruin and dust in the room made it difficult for Fritz to search through the scattered contents of the safe – but search he did.

With a torch taped to his left wrist and another strapped to his head he worked like a madman, levering with the pry-bar at the locked cash-drawer in the bottom of the safe. He counted steadily as he worked . . . twenty- four . . . twenty-five . . . twenty-six . . . none of the 'thousand' rubbish you read about in crime books and see on television to indicate seconds. That just complicates and confuses, whereas a steady count is like a hum in the background as you go about your business. Fritz had a rhythm where a count of one hundred equated to one minute. He knew to count to one hundred three times, and then skedaddle out of there no matter what.

The drawer caved in to his attack, the lock broken, and in his frenzy to lever it out the entire content of the drawer was strewn across the carpet. Money, money, money! For a moment the sight of all the cash froze his count . . . but then he regained momentum by shouting a number each time he plucked a bundle off the floor and stuffed it in his rucksack!

++++

The volume of the front siren had momentarily caused a falter in my rush across the road. But after delivering three tremendous blows of the hammer, the solid wood door smashed free from its top hinge. Then the bottom hinge was quick to follow as I awkwardly struck it underhand, standing on the footpath bathed in bright street-lighting. An ululating siren directly overhead constantly blasted my ears with deafening sound.

The deadlock on the door refused to let go, acting like a hinge, as I forced the door open by thumping it repeatedly with my shoulder, until the screws finally popped out of the wood when it slammed hard against the inside wall. Taking the hammer with me, elated that it had worked as planned, I pelted down the street to the nearest driveway . . . and disappeared into the dark recesses from view.

++++

Fritz commenced his third hundred . . . eighteen . . . nineteen . . . twenty . . . as he grabbed a petty-cash tin and tried to shake it open, but it was locked, he threw it towards the door for pick-up when he fled the office. A locked bank satchel with something in it, went straight into his bag as he kicked ledgers and account books out of his way to see what lay beneath them. The paymaster's small pistol caught his eye, so that went in the bag too. His head-torch constantly cast about like a spotlight in the night, hunting for any prey of value.

++++

I threw the hammer over a fence and quickly followed, pleased to be gone from where I felt like a duck on a lake during hunting season. My heart rate gradually subsided when the darkness of the creek was reached and I could toss the heavy sledgehammer away. Panting from excitement rather than exertion, I reached the window grill and forcefully swung it out and back against the wall, the rusty hinges squealing their protest all the way. Now, all I could do was shine a torch on the window pane and wait for Fritz . . .

+ + + +

Sixty-five . . . sixty-six . . . Fritz made a decision: every square of floor-space had been kicked over twice. He was out of there! Police were racing to intercept him, and every second wasted meant they were sixty metres closer to capturing him. Sweat pouring from his every pore, his eyes stinging and pulse pounding, Fritz scooped up the cash-tin as he rushed from the office. To his chest he clutched the money-stuffed rucksack, like a starving man would a freshly baked loaf of bread.

Fritz sped along a loading bay, through a storage area, and into an ablution block where two windows were visible high up. One glowed bright from a light outside and he scrambled awkwardly onto a sink beneath it, barely able to manage the feat with both hands full. With the tin pressed between his chest and the brickwork to release his left hand, he unlatched the window and awkwardly pulled it in and up.

+ + + +

I stood there ready, with the torch-beam now pointed towards the ground away to the left of me, with my right arm extended. Fritz dropped the rucksack into my open arm, and then threw the metal box into long grass to the left of me where the torch pointed. With both his torches switched off, Fritz eased his way out the window.

Standing together in wet grass, lit by moonlight only, I helped Fritz fit the rucksack to his back. He grabbed the tin and disappeared into the night, running along an animal track towards a spot further down the creek where he would wait for me to catch up.

I reached in and pulled the window closed (with a piece of wire) until it locked itself; then slammed the grill back into place, locking it securely with the padlock to make it appear as if it had never been tampered with.

Along the same track, I loped in the footsteps of Fritz . . . the disturbing sounds of the alarms gradually fading behind me.

+ + + +

7
THE DEVICE

Gelignite bomb

THE PAST WILL BE LESS PAINFUL
IF THE PRESENT GETS BETTER

By nature, Norm was laconic and if not for his piercing blue eyes, he would be an easily forgotten person to any observer: often an hour would go by with only a half dozen words spoken by him. However, when he did open up he always made sense.

++++

"If I was you, Joe, I'd be leaving it," Norm advised. We were discussing a criminal act of some import, one I was contemplating, and I asked for his input on an aspect to help develop it further. "You haven't been out of prison long enough, so you're still emotionally and mentally boxed in."

"What the fuck is that supposed to mean?" I asked. His answer was not what I sought. It did not gel with what I wanted to hear.

"Your thoughts become clearer when out here, and not corrupted like they are inside." I waited for him to say more . . .

Frustrated, I finally snapped, "Are you going to explain that to me or not?" My train of thought had gotten lost.

"In prison, sex is on your mind a lot; do you agree?" I nodded.

He added, "And thoughts tend to spiral around women and how you'll pick one up at a club the first night out." Again, I nodded.

"But it didn't go as smooth as you planned, did it, when it came to the pick-up." I nodded, thinking, 'How did he know that?'

"Well it's the same with ideas and plans. You need to give it more time to mellow out," he went on to say. "Let reality balance you, and *then* review what you've got planned." He leant forward to add sincerity to what he had to say next. "I can tell you now by the little bits I've heard, you're out of whack; it's not the old you. From anger-driven theory in prison, to reality out here, is a dangerously long step to take."

I was unconvinced by his argument then because my mind refused to accept it. But the obstacles encountered in pursuit of my intentions, and going over his advice, were enough to slow me down to a point where I was finally forced to face up to the fact that imprisonment had seriously fucked with my head. In fact, messed with my faculties so much that I had blinkered myself perilously close to committing an act of insanity. Not discounting the fact that the crime I planned to carry out was against a scumbag and would not have seen the light of day, it would have been a death knell for me in a number of ways.

In a prisoner's world, everything is distorted or counterfeit.

Disturbed thoughts and flights of fantasy sweep constantly through the mind like wind sowing secret plans of its own; capable of masking societal rules so effectively that it becomes a false reality you believe in. Without a rock-solid belief to anchor to, or support from someone outside whom you trust implicitly, a phony world of imaginings become valid in prison. That vile insidiousness is what befell me. The therapeutic workings of time – and Norm's calm reasoning – shook me loose of my foolishness.

+ + + +

Originally, the device was not my idea: I intended to tweak the application of it to suit an Australian environment, rather than applied as it was in far off Spain where it emerged as a weapon of terror. The person who told me all about it (sadly, my memory is going; I no longer recall his name), was European and participated in an openly violent political struggle over a mountainous region in the north of Spain. He made it clear to me that his participation was always as a facilitator, never an applicator. (An explanation of those terms will follow further into the story.)

His calm inner strength, coupled with his genuine religious nature, impressed me greatly. His legs were shorter than his wiry torso and his large hands were extraordinarily strong. Prison regime never bothered him. In my mind's eye, I picture him wearing a scarf. Of course, not a real scarf but an imaginary one – duty of care in prison did not extend that far – placed there by me as a mnemonic to help recall his name. Now, I only see the scarf and have no recollection of what name it must have meant to me back then.

Their struggle to gain recognition commenced by capturing two officials of the Spanish government, followed by demands, through facilitators that the Basque region and people (of which

Scarf was one) be recognised as a legitimate political party by the Spanish government, to guarantee their release or they would be killed. By threatening their lives, they hoped to force a quick resolution.

Cruelly ignored, the abduction demands went sour and consequently the officials died. The government cynically played on the public's apathy and ignorance of the Basque plight; they only heard official condemnation, kept ignorant and unaware of the desperate cry for a separate state: so it foundered.

A campaign strategy of terror soon developed. The public would be terrorised into demanding that their government consider the Basque claim. The deadly implementation of small explosive devices doing it at a remove became the reality. A sealed metal box the size of a clenched hand was gaffer-taped to a victim's chest before released on the outskirts of a town. The first thing the distressed person did was to run to the nearest police station for help.

Forced to watch while the device was assembled and then fitted, the victim knew the box contained a small block of explosive material connected to an electrical detonator triggered by a spring-loaded plunger pressed hard against the sternum bone of the chest. It only needed enough power to be capable of penetrating flesh – like a .22 bullet. If that plunger came out more than five millimetres, the explosive force that followed would send a lethal blast of gas and shards of metal through the rib cage. A cruel act, but they were an oppressed and determined people.

A method to circumvent the lethal device eventually worked out to be – after a few publicly catastrophic failures – a thin blade insinuated between the flesh and plunger to hold it back, before removal of the tape. The next victim carried a new twist introduced to the device: the plunger was super-glued to his chest!

As touched on earlier, the Basques' primary intention was to terrorise their opposition into compliance, and they set about doing that by selectively killing public figures in a violent way. The Spanish government responded adversely to that by hunting down known members of the group and killing them.

By chance a less violent and more profitable outcome quickly developed. Some of the victims in their terror had offered large payments in a desperate attempt to buy their way out of dying. According to Scarf, a change in Basque tactics quickly occurred. Money and information became the new objective, and the victims themselves would provide both. They set about gathering intelligence on who controlled the purse strings within the opposition, and not only money but arms and explosives too.

Scarf in his cell of three facilitators compiled a short list of names, passed over to a cell of applicators – the ruthless experts who made and fitted the devices – with a victim finally selected. Presumably, they carried out the abduction without a hitch; Scarf only made mention of the fact that it failed miserably when it came to collecting the cash. Apparently, the first victim fitted with the newly-adapted device fled straight to the authorities, willing to place his own life in police hands, even though the Basques had assured him of his freedom when he returned with the ransom money. It took the police two days to remove the super-glued device without it exploding, and when they did it successfully, it became a massive propaganda exercise.

The next victim they snatched wore an almost identical device, only this one had a cunning modification added: a simple clock mechanism, to limit the time needed by the authorities to outwit the super-glued plunger. With a dozen or so tiny holes drilled in one side of the box, a toothpick inserted into only one of them would safely open a relay inside the bomb. The only relay *not* connected into the detonating circuitry. They bluntly told the victim, if delayed reaching a pre-arranged handover point within four hours, irrespective of whether the plunger was neutralised or not, the timer inside would stop ticking and the box would detonate. The only way the victim could survive was by cooperating, and not going to the authorities, until after payment and the safe removal of the device.

According to Scarf, instead of killing numerous innocent people, many of the captured opposition were forced to pay after the device had been fitted to them, naming others in their ranks with unrevealed wealth as future victims as well as information about those who secretly held influential positions within their fold, before being released, humiliated. The financing of their struggle grew.

The war for independence apparently went on and on for years. A hardnosed insurgency according to Scarf, until the Spanish government eventually recognised that the Basque people had a legitimate claim to a separate state. After that, Scarf migrated to Australia and when I met him in Boggo Road Prison, he was serving a short sentence for shoplifting.

+ + + +

8
WOODEN BOX

Naval binoculars

THE ONLY PERSON WHO NEVER MAKES A MISTAKE IS THE PERSON WHO NEVER DOES ANYTHING

Shifty always acted like he was doing something shifty, even when he wasn't, hence his name. So when he came to me and said that he had two weeks of surveillance to do on a place I almost laughed in his face. But then he showed, by asking me to set the cameras up for him, that he understood he had a problem when it came to blending in. I agreed to do it by asking what it involved.

In the telling, Shifty said he would pay me two grand for two weeks or I could come in on the job and get an equal share. He said it would probably take about a year to complete, but involved working with an associate of Shifty who was unknown to me. So I chose cash in hand as the best choice; who knew where I might be that far down the track?

The reason Shifty approached me is that I owned state-of-the-art surveillance gear purchased directly from Japan: a scanner loaded with every police and security frequency used across the state, capable of tracking local radio traffic between dispatch and vehicle; night vision binoculars used by the Japanese navy; a few sets of walkie-talkies; and most importantly, two compact movie cameras – all available to rent for a price with a bond paid up front in the event of loss or breakage.

Four days after doing as asked, I got to see the whole picture of what was going down when Shifty reappeared at my front door quite agitated complaining that the tape viewer he held had broken down, and would I fix it immediately. Taking it from him I quickly found that the tape had unravelled and jammed the mechanism. By cutting out that piece and splicing the tape back together I got to see what had been recorded that day.

Shifty had hours of vision from where the hidden cameras in nearby trees had recorded the foundations of three buildings nearing completion on a property on the eastern outskirts of Melbourne. Each camera could take four hundred grabs, a few dozen frames automatically every fifteen minutes until the tape was full. (No such luxuries of an SD card or memory-stick back in the 70s.)

Shifty was paranoid of being remembered by the workmen if he kept turning up each day to follow construction, or seen and reported by the visiting night-watchman if he snuck around in the dark. So each morning at dawn, Shifty walked through the trees to exchange the tapes without ever being close to the brightly lit construction site. Plus, on the vision, I spotted a person walking around the site which convinced me that Shifty was wise to avoid being seen. This guy was head and shoulders worse than any 'tough' cop could ever dream of being – he would hunt down and try to bury Shifty if he found out what was going down. I commented on the risk he was taking and warned him to keep this in mind when the second half of the job was pulled.

"He's rolling in dough. I just intend to spread his wealth around a bit more evenly." Shifty was as tough as him; just not as callous.

"Yeah, I'm okay with that," I said. "But how does watching get you his money?"

"He's submitted three building plans this year to council which I got a look at," he explained. "And one of those buildings has got a security room in it; thicker walls than a bank vault."

My ears immediately pricked up. Not because of what might end up in that room, but the word vault always reminds me that I once failed dismally trying to breach one in a bank. To my chagrin the alarm system did not only protect the door as I believed; it had wires running through the walls and even the ceiling and floor to protect its integrity. My curiosity wanted to know more.

Three days later, Shifty visited me with a tape from the day before in hand. Watching it together on my big screen I quickly understood the wisdom of recording it as he pointed out salient features on the screen. The far building was obviously going to be an open shed of some kind and the one nearest would be horse stables set up with rooms all over the place. The concrete slab for a house had already been poured between the two. On close study the wood and metal formwork for one of the rooms in the stable was three times the thickness of what a normal footing would be. I asked Shifty what he intended to do at this stage, because frankly I was a bit confused by it all. He said that he intended no offence, but it might be better if he didn't tell me just yet.

"The walls and floor will be concrete as you can see," he began. "And I suppose the roof of the building will be steel girders and tin."

I nodded my agreement, adding, "But the ceiling of that room will be solid concrete, for sure."

"Of course it will be, Joe. But the walls have to be poured first to support it, before the poles with the plates on top go inside." Shifty had been a construction worker in Melbourne with the BLF during the building boom in the 60's, and so he knew each step.

"This site will be finished in a matter of months," I observed. "You said a year from now it would be done and I don't see how that can be."

"A proactive step now will guarantee success next year," Shifty cryptically stated, very sure of himself. "Are you sure you don't want in?" he asked for the last time.

I gave it due consideration before answering, "Thanks, mate, but no thanks. Are you going to enlighten me or not?" I was still very curious.

He never divulged sufficient information for me to reason out from his surveillance activity what he intended. I figured knowledge empowers, so just knowing where the strongroom was located served a purpose by keeping the planned break-in focused.

Two days later Shifty returned my equipment with a Cheshire smile on his face as I returned his bond, without any additional information forthcoming. Not long after that, Shifty drifted out of my life.

✦ ✦ ✦ ✦

A decade later I met Shifty by chance in an Adelaide restaurant and we talked about old times. By coincidence, the man I had recognised on that site had only recently been gunned down in Melbourne. So of course I touched on his activity back when I had set up the cameras for him.

"Did you do it like you said you would?" I asked.

"Yeah, mate. We got eighty grand back then, and a shit load of pills. I lived in Brisbane after that." During our conversation I soon realised that his personality had changed to one of dourness.

"If I could have it over again," he confided, "I'd never have taken the shit. The pills were a bad batch, you know." By just listening to him ramble I knew that to be an indisputable fact. Eating the fruit of his crime had obviously made him a casualty.

Drugs were the deciding factor of why I had kept out of it.

By the end of the evening Shifty had told me what I wanted to know. How he had gained entry into that seemingly impregnable concrete strongroom. It was quite simple really and only involved the use of a large engineer's hammer and a small pry bar. He and his accomplice had picked the exact night preceding the concrete pour for the walls, knowing that concreters always strove to have their formwork finished before knocking off for the night, ready to be poured in the morning.

While his mate sat concealed in the darkened trees listening on my police scanner and keeping binocular watch on the entry road through the surrounding paddocks, Shifty hefted a wooden box and slung a bag of tools over his shoulder, heading for the site. Once there he easily located the steel-plated wall he sought and dumped the box and tools at his feet before plugging his two-way bud into his ear.

Using two spanners and a tyre-lever he soon removed one of the large greasy plates bolted to each other to form the outside wall of the strongroom. Revealed inside was a triple layer of steel mesh inserted to strengthen the concrete, and impede illegal entry if thieves tried to break in. But most important of all (my nemesis years earlier) were the randomly-distributed wire-bearing conduits waiting to be connected to an alarm box yet to be fitted. Grasping a pair of small bolt-cutters, Shifty quickly cut and removed three sections of the steel mesh; but not the two conduits he saw. He pushed them aside.

In less than an hour, the wooden box he had carried to the site sat snug inside the formwork, securely wired into place three centimetres away from the inside and outside plates. The conduits containing alarm wires had been forced under and over the box. Shifty commenced replacing the outside steel plate, earlier removed by him.

(When the pour went ahead in the morning as planned, the concrete would flow around, under and over the box, until it became completely sealed in concrete, undetectable when the plates were removed a day later.) Contacting his mate to ensure that it was clear for him to exit, Shifty sped from the site and quickly located and inserted a blank tape into each camera. He needed that final bit of vision to confirm that the concrete pour went to completion without the box being detected.

That box waited a year for Shifty, like a snuggled up bear in hibernation, until the night a large hammer fractured that concrete skin to reveal the hollow wooden box buried inside.

+ + + +

9
GUNS FOR SALE

Glock 19

THREE FORCES RULE THE WORLD:
STUPIDITY, FEAR, GREED

- Albert Einstein

After greeting a friend at the front door and inviting him in, he limped ahead of me down the passage of my house to the kitchen. At the fridge he grabbed a beer before sitting at the table and, without any preamble, pulled a large pistol from his belt and placed it in front of where I was about to sit. He said it had a firing problem and would I take a look at it.

When stalking a pig in the bush a few days earlier, the gun had failed to fire at a critical moment resulting in an injury when the pig took a bite at his leg. The pistol had also failed to fire a few times previously when shooting targets, but it had not bothered him enough to get it fixed, until now. Having had some experience restoring collectable firearms, I agreed to look at it while he drank my beer.

By testing the magazine spring and removing the slide to get at the firing-pin spring, the fault and the probable cause was confirmed after asking a few pertinent questions; but a problem not so easily solved. He had always kept the magazine fully loaded and the pistol was armed more often than not, he said. Gun springs should be rested regularly, and consequently by being kept under constant compression the springs had gradually weakened over time. They needed to be replaced, similar to replacing worn-out springs on a car. But this pistol, being an unlicensed firearm, could not be taken to a gunsmith as easily as one could take a car to a servo to have new springs fitted. The simple replacement of those fatigued springs now posed a real problem.

After hearing from me a shifty way of how to go about obtaining the correct spring kit, he said it was too much trouble for him to bother and did I want to buy the gun. It was a 9 mm and stamped 'Made in Czechoslovakia' and after assuring me that he had owned it for four years, I felt comfortable enough with its provenance to say, "I'll buy it, if the price is right" and cheekily added, "provided you throw in a box of bullets as well." We agreed on a price and I took possession of it that day.

Two days later, when he returned with a box and a half of 9mm for me I asked him what he was now going to do for sport. He surprised me when he said, "Pig shooting. I luv that shit!"

"With a rifle?" I asked. "I didn't think you had one."

"I don't. I'm buying another pistol," he said. "There's a Glock for sale, going cheap."

My radar instantly went on red alert, recalling an overheard conversation eighteen months earlier. "There's no such thing as a cheap Glock!" I immediately stated: "Unless it's worn-out or red-hot."

"Nah, mate," he was quick to explain. "This one's still numbered and comes in its own box." Meaning the gun was virtually new and with its serial numbers still intact, unlikely to have been stolen or used in a serious crime.

That information made me even more suspicious, prompting me to inquire, "And how did it get here?" (meaning how did it reach the street). Invariably, cheap handguns are imported rather than expensive home-sourced ones, to maximise the profit. The price of a new Glock purchased legitimately from a gun-shop was already at the top of the black-market asking-price for a throwaway!

"I dunno," he answered, "maybe the seller's a legit owner who knows he'll get double the price for it hot – telling the cops someone stole it – than what he'd get selling it back to a gun-shop."

"Well I think you should be *real* careful buying this one," I advised him. "Two years back, I know for a fact, some Glock pistols were put on the street by the police."

"I heard a rumour about that; but so what if a bent cop sells a gun or two? They change hands all the time. And you've sold guns too."

"Yeah, but mine were always reconditioned oldies, stolen local, or imported cheapies. I guaranteed the history of every gun I ever sold. Anyone who can afford the three grand for a Glock will hang on to it, and dump their old one to cover some of the cost like you're doing. And that's where the risk is."

"What do ya mean?"

"Whoever buys a Glock, that's who the gun most likely will stay with; do you agree?"

"You're fucking paranoid. How does that help the cops?"

I then told him the gist of the conversation I had overheard between two firearm dealers at the Melbourne Gun Show. It alluded to the probability of a police sting carried out six months earlier to deliver doctored handguns to a major drug importer/manufacturer in country Victoria. Coincidently at the time when a gangland war was developing, which later resulted in a number of murders.

Quite a bit of my reasoning was conjecture, but based on a firm belief that certain police will not hesitate to set aside the rules of engagement when it becomes political or expedient to do so. By matching the five points a discharged pistol leaves at the scene of a crime, a unique forensic fingerprint exists which can later be conclusively matched to the firearm which did the firing. And if that firearm happens to be in the possession of a known criminal, even if the weapon is later destroyed, the investigating police have an immediate starting point, if not a firm suspect.

"Forensic would link it all together," I explained, "giving a cop invaluable knowledge when interrogating the person who originally purchased the pistol, working forward from there." (The reason informers are so vital during investigations – and why dubious deals are constantly done – is they give information and clues to the police, leading to possible suspects.) In this case a recovered piece of lead or a spent bullet-case at a crime scene would do exactly the same, without the informer involvement, and more certainty in the mind of an investigator in on the giggle.

"And how would they do that?" my friend jeeringly stated, having missed the point. Not for a moment believing that I had a plausible answer to his question, I went into finer detail assembling the puzzle the way I understood it: explaining how one of the gun dealers' sons who worked in the police bureau of forensics had filed test-reports on three new Glock pistols. Armed with that knowledge an investigator would appear incredibly good, like a Sherlock Holmes, to their superior and up for promotion when a shooter or a murderer was quickly tracked.

"That doesn't make any sense, Joe: forensic comes *after* a criminal event."

"Not if the gun was forensically tested *before* being sold," I quickly asserted, "and the seller is an undercover cop or informer willing to testify that it was sold to you." That stopped him mentally: it was obvious he had never considered it from that angle. His next statement confirmed his comprehension.

"If a forensic report for a crime matched a *secret* profile they already had, it *would* identify a gun," and on a rising note, he exclaimed, "and they'd know where to begin!" His brow furrowed as the realisation of the deviousness sunk in.

I quickly added, "I'm not suggesting the Glock you want has that smell about it. But how could you ever be sure?" I could see the anger in his face developing, and knowing him and his willingness to punch people, I figured the seller would be in for a torrid time if I didn't intercede. Plus, if the pistol had already been used in a violent crime and was being stupidly sold instead of destroyed, would it muddy the investigation enough to be worth the risk of selling it on to a person who would never inform on how he came by it?

"I have a simple solution though, provided you don't blow the sale." I smiled confidently as I added, "For a hundred bucks I'll make it a virgin again." He stared at me while he processed my offer.

"Yeah, I'm interested," he finally said. "But how are you going to do that?"

At the time of telling I didn't go into great detail, but said enough to satisfy my friend that I knew what I was talking about. Two days later he turned up carrying a small flat box: before he even opened it to display what it held, I knew it would be a

Glock, a gun I had never handled before.

"Leave it with me and I'll give you a call tomorrow." After some small talk over a beer, he left me to it.

I soon discovered how complicated a handgun of that quality is and how difficult its maintenance would be for anyone outside the legitimate gun owners loop. Fortunately a manual came with the gun: without it, I might not have been able to reassemble it, let alone 'fix' the gun as promised!

When a bullet (or in legalese, a projectile) is recovered at a crime scene, it bears markings unique to the barrel which directed it on its way. Some barrels have five, six, or even seven helical grooves cut in the steel for the lead or copper jacket to lock into when the bullet is fired. And as it accelerates down the barrel those grooves rotate the projectile at least once so that by the time it leaves the barrel a millisecond after being fired at a target, it is spinning through the air making it far more accurate than a tumbling ball. Of course by doing so, the bullet becomes a powerful informant uniquely marked by the end of the grooves as it erupts from the muzzle.

The second and most damning piece of evidence is the bullet-case; which is why savvy criminals invariably use revolvers, and not copy movie thugs firing semi-automatics turned on their side. A case ejected by a pistol as it self-loads another round into the chamber provides more pieces of unique evidence when viewed under a powerful microscope, evidence which will help seal the fate of the shooter in court.

Five actions happen, in less time than an eye-blink. But when slowed down they are individual and in sequence, each leaving indelible evidence of their passing. Reacting to the compelling force after a bullet is fired, the slide is propelled back as far as it will go, compressing the firing pin spring and simultaneously extracting the empty case and ejecting it. The compressed mainspring propels the slide forward again to chamber the next round, but in doing so, the firing pin is held back by the sear, a small component which traps the firing pin once its spring is compressed. The flange which held the bullet in the magazine scrapes the brass as it is forced out of the magazine and into the chamber (one), and the slide which drives the bullet into the chamber also leaves an identifiable mark (two). Now the pistol is armed, ready to be fired again.

When the trigger is squeezed it releases the sear. The firing pin is driven forward with such force, it detonates the tiny primer cap seated centrally in the rear of the bullet (three) igniting the main cordite charge inside the bullet-case. And within a millisecond after the projectile has left the barrel, the pistol recoils from the kick of the explosive as the slide is driven back by the empty case firmly gripped by the extractor (four) to the ejection port where it is flicked out (five) and flung to a place metres away where some diligent investigator will later locate it.

A revolver leaves none of that, the brass informants that forensic love to find stay in the cylinder. And a light file of the revolver's muzzle changes everything back to new again. Admittedly the filing of the muzzle will affect accuracy if carelessly done, but only a target shooter would notice the difference.

The next day, entirely satisfied with my handiwork, I handed back my mate's gun telling him he could continue his favourite sport of stalking feral pigs. The worry of not knowing where the gun came from – now *totally* clean with the serial numbers drilled out – was no longer an issue.

+ + + +

10
PROACTIVE

A cash-security safe

IF YOU CAN'T EXPLAIN IT SIMPLY,
YOU DON'T UNDERSTAND IT WELL ENOUGH

Friday night in Melbourne with groups of young partygoers rushing by, I stood with a mate, Tom, in front of a Swanston Street arcade peering at the plaque that listed the business names of those in the building. We were there to suss out a particular business. It was a payment centre for quite a few Melbourne city rentals, paid fortnightly according to Tom. And CBD rentals did not come cheap. The few crumbs of information he imparted had intrigued me sufficiently to hook my criminal interest.

+ + + +

"See that," he said; "see that safe in there?"

I swung my head to peer more closely through the front glass window of an estate agent's office on the ground floor. The safe inside was a modern Chubb less than ten years old; it squatted in the corner of the room behind an ornate wooden desk with a small cabinet to one side. Only the top section of the safe was visible to anyone like us interested in looking in from outside, but strangely the door had been left open, allowing me to confirm by the position of the locking bolts and the thickness of the door that it was an expensive security model specifically designed to protect large sums of money (and thwart tankmen) and not one of the more commonly used cheaper commercial types manufactured to protect small amounts of cash, or more particularly documents, in the event of a fire.

"Yeah, it's a safe; so what?" I replied. "Is this what you brought me here to see?" I felt disappointed, angry with myself, thinking that I had wasted my time and travelled to the CBD for nothing. I growled, "You said it was a goer." Safes were my criminal interest, but I knew this one was beyond my safe-cracking abilities and it pissed me off that he had brought me here.

"It's a goer, mate. It is," he enthused. "I'm telling you my idea will work."

"Yeah, and you haven't yet told me what that is," I quickly snapped back, cutting into him. "It's not a game of poker. The door's wide open, so unless someone forgot to lock it, I'm guessing there's not much money in there." I figured the safe had been left open to indicate to any lurking tankman that breaking in would not be worthwhile, garnering nothing but petty-cash from the locked drawers of the safe and worthless bookkeeping materials.

"That's why I wanted you to see it first, Joe, before I said anything. If we come here over the weekend, it'll still be open, but if we come back during the week it's locked every day. I've been watching." His next sentence triggered an instant hunch of where he was heading with this venture. "Is this one of those safes you told me about, Joe, where the combination can be changed from inside the door?"

In our local pub's beer garden only a month or so before this reconnaissance, I had explained to Tom how modern security safes are designed so that their initial combination can be changed by the owner after purchase for satisfaction of mind, or if it becomes known or suspected at any time that someone unauthorised might have learnt the magic numbers. On the inside of a safe's door for that purpose, directly behind the combination, a small door is fitted: of course that trap is invariably locked, and the key is kept safely somewhere else as recommended by the safe people. Even key-controlled safes have a similar safeguard; often it is just an affixed panel easily removed by a locksmith (or an intrepid thief) with the correct tools to allow swapping of the lock-box, or the cheaper option of changing a ward or two in the event that a different key is required, though obviously not as easily accessed as a locked trap.

The people who used this safe had outsmarted themselves. Leaving the safe open telegraphed when it held money (Monday through to Friday afternoon, when the rental payments were taken out and banked) plus, by unwittingly providing the means to unlock their safe, this job would be an 'open sesame' for a proactive thief in the early hours of Friday morning. They were dumber than the clever-dick car owners who conceal a back-up key somewhere under their vehicle in the event they lose or misplace the one they carry. *Every* auto thief with a smidgen of intelligence knows to spend ten minutes of their idle time giving a vehicle a thorough once-over search for a concealed key before going to the trouble of breaking in and stealing it.

A safe of this quality is virtually impregnable when the door is kept constantly locked as it is supposed to be – not foolishly left open to be taken advantage of by any observant thief with minimal break-and-enter skills, who should be capable enough to unlock the small inner door with a lock-pick or a bump key, then record the sequence of numbers visible on the combination wheels inside the door.

Tom and I would need to explore the building to find a way in – even a direct assault through the front was a possibility – and afterwards think a bit on how to intrude without leaving visible evidence of our entry (and exit) after getting the combination. Then patiently wait till the right Thursday night to re-enter, but this time to spin the stolen numbers on the combination dial on the front of the securely-locked safe!

If carried out, its success would lay hidden in its misleading simplicity: and I intended to carry it out. The police would surely conduct their investigation into the robbery on the basis that it was an inside job with the combination being used to enter the safe, and not search beyond the business staff for the culprit. My evening in the city picked up: it had not been a waste of time for me after all.

"Let's go to a city pub, Tom," I chortled. "Tonight's drinks are on me."

+ + + +

11
THE ENTERTAINER

ALEXANDRA the GREAT "48"

A HUNGRY BELLY IGNORES GOOD SENSE

- Joe Tog

Alexandra was a sensational cabaret entertainer, a Sophia Loren look-alike, with a statuesque body and breasts the size of footballs (hence her stage name) and I am not exaggerating. They really were humungous. She strutted into Pentridge Prison one Sunday morning radiating vitality in a fashionable mini-dress and knee-high white leather boots – on each flank a prison warder dressed in navy blue escorted her. Alexandra was a real woman, a rare sight in prison in '74.

In small groups clustered around each heavily-barred window in the chapel upstairs of B-division, we stared out with mouths agape in amazement as she headed towards us, the toughest division in Pentridge, a guard-tower and overhead catwalk framed behind her. Her roadies and two-man band had already trouped in an hour before and were set up on the small stage where just a few hours earlier Fr Brosnan, the prison chaplain, had conducted mass. The men in the chapel – now filled to overflowing with a diversity of inmates escorted in from many of the other divisions – were antsy with anticipation and the buzz of lively conversations rising and falling blocked outside sounds. Nevertheless, through it all, I heard my name called.

Dodging muscled-up and tattooed bodies and stepping over feet, I weaved back to my seat, held by a friend besieged by an aggressive two demanding my spot, to claim my central position two rows in from the stage. Front row seats are of course the best, but they accommodated the prisoner (and his privileged friends) who once worked in the entertainment industry and had organised this unbelievable event. He sat front and centre basking in the glow of a job well done – and deservedly so. The decade of the rebellious and riotous 70s had introduced many improvements into prison, but this was an astounding first in entertainment!

"Fuck off, this is mine!" I asserted the moment I reached my seat. "Do you think a seat sits empty just for you?" I got a couple of nasty stares, but not enough to deter me from sitting down and enjoying the moment.

The MC came out and asked for our attention. The microphone hissed and the volume was too loud, but everyone instantly listened up. No one in the audience really knew what to expect, except maybe the organiser but he was not letting on. Prison officers, with their regulation hats on, stood around the edge of the assembly, twelve or so blue uniformed types with a couple of security screws dressed in black at the rear standing against the walls either side of the open steel-gated entry/exit. As the MC talked, during a lull in the telling of a joke, I heard the clank of a key turning the lock. No prisoner could enter or leave now until the show ended.

The music started and the harsh glare of the overhead fluorescent lights blinked out casting all into shadow, everyone faintly lit by the sunlight streaming in through six large windows, three down each side of the room. Two spotlights came on and lit the stage as the music grew louder, from a low background rhythm to a rapid, in your face, drum roll. Then magically Alexandra appeared, stepping out from a small curtained area that concealed a door (used by the priest when entering from a secure office area below).

A clamour of clapping and cheering welcomed Alexandra as she commenced a dance routine, attired in colourful clothes, red high heels, and shoulder length auburn hair. The packed room of men were mesmerised. Within twenty minutes, (they said the show lasted an hour, but it felt much shorter) she had stripped down to a spotted leotard and heels, running off risqué jokes while miming coitus throughout the telling. Depending on how you viewed it, the show went rapidly downhill after that.

I was in a sweat, a real bother, and I saw a few nearby were far worse off – and it had nothing to do with the warm spring weather outside or the fug in the room steamed up by excited males. What the deviants in the room must have been doing while this went on, I refused to contemplate. Criminals from every alleyway and occupation surrounded me.

I thought the striptease was pretty much over, reached its end, but when the leotard came off next, I sat gobsmacked. Even though I was twenty-six, I had never been to a full-on strip show. Only three licensed venues operated in Melbourne back in the 70s: two in Saint Kilda and one in the CBD. Alexandra wore the skimpiest of panties and a silken bra the same colour as her skin, with the nipple area prominently pushed out. I focused on her every move, free of prison intrigues and mindset, with no lasting memory of what she may have said, profound or otherwise. She held the shoulder straps of her brassiere undone in her hands, ready to pull the cups away. She did a whirl and a few fancy dance steps, full of vigour, teasing the audience. The entire mass of men sat enthralled, when the music in the speakers gave another drum roll – she lifted the cups slowly away and let her breasts swing free. They jiggled voluptuously, and the roar of approval by two hundred prisoners confirmed our puerile appreciation. The bra ended up in the centre of the audience, flung there as she whirled across the small stage, a brief scuffle for ownership and gruff words the only discordant sound as she danced on. I gazed quickly around at the commotion, trying to gauge the feeling of the room: on a precipice of sexual emotion, but not about to lose control. However, in that look I also caught a glimpse of a Chief Warden at the back of the room remove his hat and wipe his brow with a handkerchief as he whispered intently to the young officer standing beside him. That screw left him and quickly edged his way along the wall towards the stage.

A ripple of excited shock coursed through me and I swung back to watch as a hundred throats roared, an animal growl really, full of passion and loss as Alexandra teased the room with the elastic top of her panties gripped, as though ready to reveal all. Two older screws standing close to the stage saw the younger warder lunge forward with his hand up in a stop sign to put a halt to the removal of the final piece of apparel but fortunately – correctly interpreting the volatile nature of the audience – both screws exercised wiser heads and were quick to grab an arm each and detain him. If he had succeeded in interrupting the show with such a finale promised, as I am *sure* they knew, a riot would have ensued! Besides, I think those two standing so close to the action on the stage watching Alexandra prance about were as temporarily besotted as any of us.

She stepped out of her panties in one lithe movement without missing a beat – perfectly aware of what had just occurred by her glance to the struggling screw – and flung them dead centre into the front row. A hundred or more pairs of excited feet stamped the floorboards to a crescendo as she grasped a breast in each hand and twirled her large nipples in opposing circles to the musical beat, her feet spread wide.

After that, there was no stopping her. I am certain Alexandra breached a swag of morality laws for us that day, caught up in the same magic; she even bent over as a final gesture with her bum towards us and did a few toe touches with her feet spread wide. Half the men in that room would have jumped off a cliff for her if she had asked – myself included – and the other half would callously have pushed a substitute.

I was traumatised for life (not true, but I have struggled with a breast fetish since then) and *everybody* raved about her raunchy performance for months to those unfortunate to have missed her show, long after Alexandra had left us to 24/7 prison drudgery.

+ + + +

Postscript:

Researching the background of Alexandra decades later, after writing the above story from memory alone, I learnt the truth about my naivety. Alexandra was the stage name of Gayle Sherman, both female names adopted after undergoing a sex change in the 60s. Her defiance flaunted in the face of authority for all to see – forever banned from performing in any Victorian prison for such blatant impudence – still impresses me to this day.

+ + + +

12
ESCAPE

Gate control catwalk in Pentridge: administration building in the background

STEADY, STEADY . . . WINS EVERY TIME

-Joe Tog

He said it could be done and when Aitch said it could, I believed him. He was a hard man in his late thirties, about 80 kilos, and stood 174 centimetres. After all it was his neck being put on the chopping-block, not mine. When he asked for assistance I remarked I would be happy to help (pleased in fact), given an opportunity to stick it up the Victorian prison system. Aitch had plans to escape from maximum security, B-Division, Pentridge. And he said he only had eight days to do it in.

I asked facetiously, "How come you've got so many days?" alluding to the fact that some escape attempts took months to put in place, even years. "Are you sure it can't be done quicker than that?" my scepticism plain to hear.

Aitch just looked at me. "The roof on the admin block is being repaired. And the worker I spoke with said it was a ten-day job. That was two days ago."

"What! You've already worked out a plan based on that?" It didn't completely surprise me that he had done as stated, the tiniest change in security patterns or prison procedure being instantly noticed: but to go out through the front of the prison *was* a bit of a challenge, to say the least. But as Aitch had often quoted, 'Luck favours a prepared mind'. Five years earlier in the Central District Courts of Melbourne he'd been convicted of two brutal murders and sentenced to hang (in the early 70s) but because of the controversial nature of Ronald Ryan's hanging a few years earlier in the late 60s the Victorian government commuted his death penalty to a sentence of fifty years, with a forty year minimum before parole. His extraordinarily harsh sentence was also an additional incentive.

The administration block was the stolid face Pentridge presented to the world. It stretched at least a hundred metres parallel to Champ Street, Coburg. Built entirely from prison-quarried, hand-hewn bluestone blocks, it stood two stories high with a battlemented parapet topping its entire length. Central to the front, an imposing clock tower reared on one side of the main gate and on the other side of that gate an almost identical tower bearing a sturdy communication mast. Two guards, each with holstered revolvers on their hips, plus an M1 30-calibre carbine racked in each tower, were posted with other staff inside the vehicle checkpoint protected by a reinforced portcullis roller-door. The towers were built into the outside wall displaying medieval gunports in the shape of Christian crosses, with a concealed catwalk above the gate so that if attacked from outside guards equipped with carbines could cover the two entry points below. All windows looking over the street, and inside the prison, were heavily barred. Joined by a five metre high wall of bluestone blocks, the first and last tower of eighteen, which encircled the forty hectare prison property, perched atop the walls near each end of the building, their glass panes glittering in sunlight like multi-eyed squatting beasts. Forty metres inside the prison, an exclusion wall five metres high enclosed the entirety of the administration building to keep prisoners at bay in the event of being besieged from within. An internal overhead guard tower and catwalk straddled a divided vehicle gate in the wall below it, as well as a pedestrian gate, for all traffic to and from the inner sanctum of the prison. Seventy metres either side of the internal road entry the wall turned back and joined the outside wall where those beast-like towers sat. A seemingly impregnable bastion, one would think. Plus no one, absolutely no one, could pass through that gate towards the administration building without producing an up-to-date and signed movement-slip for the perusal of the catwalk guard above; unless they were under escort, or dressed in a blue uniform. During the previous year five determined breakouts had been attempted and all had failed. Not one of those five attempts had been prepared to take on the admin building. And *this* was the way Aitch picked to go!?

I quickly recruited my best mate, Bomber, and brought him up to speed on the plan. His brash nature would add to the potential success of it, with me and three others from other divisions already recruited by Aitch to complete the group needed to get him out.

It was an audacious, as well as a deadly, endeavour for Aitch, if the plan ran off track and went haywire, with disgruntled guards willing to shoot at the first hint of an escape attempt. (For some prison officers tower duty was assigned as a form of punishment.) The Ryan and Walker break-out only ten years before, when a prison guard was shot dead while they made good their escape in a commandeered car, was clear in all of our minds. Aitch was a loyal friend but, to be absolutely honest when describing his character under the pressure of a B-division riot we went through together, he was an unforgiving bastard: with nerves of steel and implacable when the going got tough.

Always proactive, Aitch already had eight metres of cloth rope stashed away. During the previous year he had secretly woven it from hundreds of short lengths of bindings he had gathered from rolls of material delivered every month to his assigned workshop where prison clothing was produced. Attached to a small grappling hook made from prison issue belt buckles, and wrapped in plastic, it lay buried deep in an A-division garden bed kept for just such an unlikely eventuality, watched over by an inmate in that less security-hostile sector of the prison. We were in B-division, the maximum security building where all the prison baddies were kept: subject to stricter rules, under constant surveillance, and constantly subjected to spot searches. If kept there, the rope would long ago have been unearthed by zealous screws.

✦ ✦ ✦ ✦

Day six:

A screw escorted me to the tailor shop, where Aitch worked on a sewing machine, to get a rip in my shirt sewn up, and while there unbeknown to the escort we exchanged contraband: a small bottle of Indian ink from me (used by inmates for tattooing) while from him I took possession of a squishy piece of yeast (vital for brewing wine) to pay the ink-trader who worked with me in the wire-netting shop. Aitch would use that ink to colour a pair of pants, being made out of grey-striped mattress material, into black. While there, after a reassuring look around to be sure the screws and the overseer were not watching, he revealed a red shirt, beautifully made with cuffs and a pointed collar: an excellent measure of his tailoring ability. The shirt he intended to wear when escaping.

+ + + +

Day five:

A practice trip from the workshops to the medical rooms (known unanimously as the 'vet run') was done to coordinate with the A-division guy to be sure we had it right. Every working day at around 9.30 am an escort screw came to each workshop gate and yelled out for those who had earlier put their name down to see the doctor on a list in each division. As the screw returned from the wire-netting workshop with me, I watched the prisoners being gathered up, along with Bomber and Aitch. There were eight of us.

Normally a movement-slip is mandatory whenever a prisoner goes from one place to another. Only a correctly dated slip with your name on it and signed by a senior person in authority can ensure you passage and if ever lost in transit, you are in *big* trouble! But in this case, when a group of prisoners is being moved and remains under escort, names are not required, just a count of how many went, and another count to ensure the same number of prisoners return. Aitch relied on that weakness in the system.

After standing in two lines of four like an army squad, being counted twice at the security box and frisked before leaving workshop alley, we were ordered to keep bunched up as we marched (if you could call it that) up the bitumen road towards the administration building. We travelled quickly, at least six hundred metres or more exchanging gossip, past the kitchen and

C-division on our right, with the clothing store and boiler-house on our left. Passing B-division on our left and E-division on our right, directly ahead of us I could see through the gates below the overhead tower into the central portal under the clock and mast tower.

Without the leading two inmates needing to be told they swung right, following a bitumen path between two flowering garden beds towards the entry into the building snigged in between the tower wall and the end of E-division. We had arrived at the medical complex which housed the dentist, doctor, and a small recovery room. The whole trip had been an adventure, rather than a chore, now that excitement was sensed in the air.

About fifteen inmates were already there in a queue waiting. Aitch forged his way to the front, jumping the line with no one complaining once they saw that both Bomber and I were right behind him. Those who were prison-smart realised that some kind of game was in play (queue jumping was frowned upon) so remained silent, and we reached the front unchallenged. Leaving Aitch at the front of the line, Bomber and I retreated happy to be the last called, giving us ample time to scope out our role needed to be played in a few days' time.

Our part in the escape, when it came, was to distract the overhead catwalk screw so that Aitch, if he successfully passed the first hurdle and was allowed through the pedestrian gate, could begin his escape attempt in earnest and unobserved.

While Bomber and I discussed tactics and worked out view-lines to later pass on to Aitch, the sick parade from A-division arrived under escort as expected. I didn't know who was to bring the rope on the day for Aitch, but I assumed he would be doing a practice run like us. And sure enough, as soon as Aitch came out he located and introduced us to his other accomplice, Dale, the person who would fill in for him in our escort group after he disappeared. When the escort screw counted us at the medical centre before being marched back to our workplaces, it was imperative that the count tallied with the number on his movement-slip. If not, it would quickly be ascertained after a name-call that Aitch was not where he should have been and the hunt would be on, with a siren blast to alert every tower guard that a high-risk prisoner had gone missing and was on the loose.

+ + + +

Day four:

It became evident that two extra screws now patrolled the work zone between the administration building and the internal wall, but that didn't seem to faze Aitch. "There's a ladder in there now, and workmen walking around," he nonchalantly stated. "I'm surprised they weren't posted there earlier."

He went on to say, "Unless I'm recognised, I'm just another stiff off the street toiling in their backyard." I felt relieved that the part I played took no great effort, whereas Aitch would be *in extremis* placing his life on the line yet he acted so casual when talking about it.

Movements of inmates from the workshops to the divisions, individually or as a group, often involved as many as three body pat-downs; but when going to the doctor it always involved only the outgoing search (another flaw in the system). Aitch took advantage of that aspect and kept his civvies − black pants and red shirt − stashed in a hollow piece of wood used as a sewing machine prop where he worked until the day they were needed. He would wear them under his prison garb, and to be sure they went undetected during that cursory search, Bomber and I had a strategy to divert the attention of the security screws conducting it.

+ + + +

Day three:

It had to be brought forward to the very next day! Aitch had got wind of the fact that additional works were going to be done in an area critical to the success of his venture. A prisoner called to the front office to collect his committal transcripts had overheard a discussion that the security chief's office located in the administration building was to be closed down for a week, and temporarily relocated to an office in B-division until the repairs had finished.

That untimely news put Aitch into a bit of a spin. The only way he knew for certain to get unimpeded movement through to the administration block was to show that he had been summoned by Security; even the screws were a bit edgy around them, and never challenged their movement orders. Aitch had gone to a great deal of effort to obtain and falsify a slip signifying that he had to attend the security office. His entire plan hinged on it.

+ + + +

The next day:

The moment I heard my name called through the gate to join the medical parade, I thought, 'Today is the day', and immediately felt nervous; not for myself, but for Aitch. In B-division that morning straight after let-out, before the official rollcall muster and count, I raced to tier six where all the lifers were held, to ascertain if Aitch had changed any of the plan for that day. He stated abstractedly that nothing more could be done. I left him sitting on his bed calmly smoking a cigarette, while I went and found Bomber.

In the workshop my job was to keep the floor clean. I swept it vigorously, cleaner than it usually got, while waiting for the expected call. When it came, I stepped out of the workshop and joined the small group of prisoners already picked up by the escort officer, and stood in line until the outside security screw had relocked the gate. And then we were marched onwards to the next shop. By the time we reached the security box (where the search and count was confirmed before leaving workshop alley) we totalled fourteen. Aitch had positioned himself midway, not knowing which end the count would be started from, giving Bomber and I time to get our charade going.

"Hey, Bomber!" I called out when the search commenced. "I heard that a pervert asked your sister if she was sexually active; and guess what she said?"

He snapped at me in simulated anger, "What the fuck are you on about?" The screw patting the guys down was two away from Aitch and seemed oblivious to what was being said, until I gave the punch-line.

"She answered, 'No mister, I just lay there'."

The screw actually laughed before comprehending how insulting to Bomber it must have been. A few other guys sniggered as well, unable to hold it in.

Bomber glared at me, saying, "You're gunna fucking get it!"

I quickly responded to his threat by adding, "Not as much as your sister is!"

He pretended to lunge at me, obliging the screw to stop his search of Aitch and order Bomber to stand back in line.

The screw then turned on me and said in no uncertain terms: "Shut up – or you'll be charged!" Aitch just stared ahead, almost as though he had been intimidated by the contretemps.

"Pete," I quickly segued to a crim not in on the joke, "Why do Irishmen wear two condoms when having sex?"

And without even waiting for him to reply, I yelled the answer in Irish brogue, "To be sure, to be sure!" Then I jokingly asked the screw, who just happened to be Irish, "Is that joke okay, officer?" A few of the men laughed openly this time, knowing it was at the screw's expense.

The screw ignored my jibe, seeing it for what it was, but left Aitch as hoped to move up and roughly frisk me in frustration, to continue the pat-downs unaware of the import of what had transpired. Bullshit always baffles those who *think* they're smart.

We marched in disorder along the central road towards the dispensary, passing all the divisions as usual; but because this was the real thing and therefore deadly serious, I recall only fleeting aspects of the trip. Aitch was ahead of me, so he constantly held my thoughts and attention. He hurried along in his usual way, though I saw his shoulders were hunched – an inner tenseness that could not be concealed.

At the medical rooms all the men broke into smaller groups to gossip with those already congregated there. We again jumped the queue as rehearsed the first time, to get Aitch in and out quickly. And when he came out, we three stood together on the bitumen near the raised garden beds which lined each side of the road just in from the gate and overhead walkway. Aitch faced the tower and the administration block, to study the screw above the gate while we talked, anxiously awaiting the arrival of Dale and the rope: Aitch couldn't begin until he had it.

Names were regularly being called for men to go in. The genuinely sick ones in the queue were being smoothly processed, so the stragglers like Bomber and me would soon be wanted. Aitch was showing stress…and then my name was called. I rushed into the clinic, leaving Bomber and Aitch isolated on the bitumen.

Clutching a tiny tube of medical toothpaste, I stepped out of the clinic (one way of obtaining reasonable toothpaste was to claim that you had sensitive teeth or sore gums) to discover that the men outside the clinic had almost doubled, the anxiously awaited A-division group had arrived and presumably the rope had been transferred over. Dale stood next to Bomber, Aitch stood alone a few metres apart from them. I made eye contact with Aitch just as the phone in the guard tower rang out loud.

Before the phone had time to ring a second time, Aitch instantly took advantage of the screw's distraction by casually crossing the road towards B-division. The moment he reached the garden beds lining the other side of the road he halted and pretended to weed the roses, manoeuvring around so that he could watch for when the screw finished his phone conversation. I could hardly bear to watch, the many ways of failure flashing through my thoughts, my heart thumping.

I chanced a look at the catwalk – the screw had finished his phone-call – and Aitch was on the move! The screw watched him as he strolled towards the gate from B-division, studying the slip of paper he now clutched in his hand for all to see. Bomber and I watched mesmerised. Only minutes away from now Aitch could be lying on the ground in handcuffs destined for punishment in H-division, slipped from the roof a broken man, or shot dead.

"Security wants me," Aitch answered in response to the question, "Where are you off to?" asked by the screw above the pedestrian gate. Aitch held the slip up high knowing all that needed to be seen were the magical words, 'Required by Security.'

The screw did not bother to take it further. He simply pulled on the appropriate lever to release the gate below. Aitch slipped through and closed the gate in the wall behind him as the rules on all controlled points required. (To have forgotten that rule would have brought down the wrath of all screws nearby.)

I didn't see what Aitch did next, though I watched him in my mind knowing what had been rehearsed. He had no choice but to enter the lion's den (through a door in the administration building which gave access to the security office) in the event the gate screw watched his progress. But on entering that area, provided he remained unchallenged, a toilet used exclusively by security screws waited as a change room to suit Aitch's needs. Once divested of his prison garb, and his beard attached (he had cunningly crafted one from the off-cuts of his own hair) a new person would emerge from the building. Aitch's heart would have been thumping.

Visualising the scene caused me to lose track of events, and I mini-panicked when returned to real time, concerned that I would fail Aitch. It was crucial that the screw's attention be drawn from his direction. I instantly whistled, and then waved at an imaginary inmate in the entrance of B-division. (Loud whistling was forbidden: it conflicted with the real whistles all screws were issued for emergency use.)

"You, prisoner!" the screw on the catwalk yelled. "What do you think you're doing?"

"I forgot, sir. Sorry, I'm sorry," I instantly responded, feigning abject apology.

"Not you!" the screw snarled at me. "Him!" and jabbed a pointed finger in another direction. Surprised, I turned my head to see.

After Aitch had passed through the gate, Bomber had commenced abusing me; I had verbally snapped back as though we might come to blows, hoping our charade would draw the screw's attention away from Aitch. But then it became a bit vague. Obviously challenged without my participation, Bomber changed tactics and went outside our script. He had reacted quicker than me.

Standing in one of the garden beds amidst the Governor's prize yellow roses, forbidden for prisoners to even touch, Bomber was eating one of the yellow blooms, while deliberately plucking a beautiful second rose from the same bush.

"Get out of them roses!" the screw cried, frustration ringing in his voice.

I burst into shocked laughter, knowing that Bomber had done *exactly* what Aitch needed, and then shouted loud enough for all to hear, including the irate screw, "He's cracked up; another one's bit the dust!"

I continued laughing as I edged away showing a callous disinterest in his pretended mental disorder. It was not uncommon. (Every month somewhere in the prison cauldron, pressure caused an inmate to melt down.)

The screw walked quickly to his telephone in the tower and made a call, all the while glaring at Bomber, watching as he stuffed the second rose into his mouth. A movement behind the catwalk on the battlemented parapet of the administration building caught my eye. I focused on it. The arms of an extension ladder extended a metre above the parapet battlements and in sight ascended a bearded person in a red shirt. My heart jumped into my mouth. Go for it, Aitch!

Inmates nearby had watched with amusement the shouted encounter with Bomber unfold, and if they noted movement on the roof like I did, I'm sure they were oblivious to its portent. To them, it would have been just another workman doing his job. I ran and grabbed Bomber, whispering hoarsely, "Aitch is on the roof! Keep going!" And then I pushed him.

Bomber threw a wild punch towards me as he staggered back. Then grabbed up a hand full of soil and threw it at me. Turning my head to avoid the dirt I took a long squizz at the roof and watched Aitch make that perilous step from the ladder rung to the parapet. In one fluid movement he stepped onto the bluestone ledge and then down a metre to stand on the slate roof inside.

As he did so, Aitch turned slightly to his right, revealing he had pinned his white movement-slip to his shirtfront where a pocket would normally have been, to vaguely resemble a mandatory visitor's tag worn by every civilian within the prison. And from a distance, his beard appeared as attached as the hair on his head. He looked exactly like a roof inspector should appear or whatever tower guards might expect a supervisor to look like!

My heart beat a wobbly rhythm as he walked his way up the slope of the roof towards the ridge. The battlemented tops of the two towers were visible from where I watched – the clock tower and the radio mast rose above them – but Aitch would not be visible from any of the deadly gunports (they were below the roofline) until he crossed over the apex to the other side of the roof…but mentally he knew. As he ascended the mossy slate, he verged right, away from the towers on his left. The test of his audacity would soon be known.

During the short space of time it took me to dodge another thrown handful of garden soil by Bomber, Aitch was no longer in sight: he had crossed over the apex of the roof and descended to the battlements on the other side. I left Bomber standing there shaking his head no longer acting foolish, and headed for the infirmary just as the medical orderly burst into sight, followed by our escort screw, in response to the tower phone call, almost colliding with me as I stepped aside and watched them hurry towards Bomber.

He stepped out of the rose bed when ordered and meekly followed the screws back into the medical centre, giving me a wink as he passed by: Bomber would certainly get some weird medication prescribed after this carry-on! And still no siren clamoured. My imagination had to be subdued.

For me, the minutes dragged by. I forced my feet to stay still: pacing up and down would have revealed my agitation, alerting screws later to the fact that I may have played a part in the escape attempt. But as the time stretched longer and longer, without a siren or hullabaloo sounding, I started to believe that Aitch may have done something incredible.

Either that or please not let it be, I thought, still on the roof with his hook and rope unable to descend to the footpath without being spotted. The best scenario was that a ladder might be propped on the outside wall of the building. All I could do was sweat drops of worry for him.

Dale, the guy who smuggled the rope up from A-division, caught my eye and gave an open-handed gesture of inquiry, indicating if Aitch had done it yet. I nodded, affirming it for him.

His casual demeanour changed. The second half of his task now came into play, and it was far riskier than bringing up the rope had been. Aitch's place had to be filled to assure being returned to our workplaces. Substituting for Aitch put him in a workshop he should not be in and if found there, the dreaded punishment division in Pentridge would be his next stop! I sympathised with what he was feeling: three times I had been sent there to break rocks, and it was no joke.

Bomber's absence worried me; he had not come back out. I had to go in and find him, even though our recent display of anger towards each other contradicted any kind of friendship. But then I thought, why should I care, all screws believed us to be nutty, unpredictable, and violent anyway. So in I strolled.

"What's going on, mate?" I asked as soon as I saw him. Relaxed back on a gurney, Bomber was reading a medical pamphlet about depression. "Are you coming back with us or what?"

"Yeah; of course I am. I'm just resting." He gave me a general rundown of his condition, and what the doctor had said. A week of rest with a visit to the prison psychiatrist in G-division had been prescribed. Satisfied that he would accompany us back, I worried less about covering for Dale. As explained earlier, when large escorts moved around the prison, individual names were rarely called after the initial pick-up. They were just expected to assemble back into their groups when they were called. But just in case, Bomber and I had to be handy in the event that Dale was required to answer to Aitch's name to avoid being detected as his substitute.

If all went as planned, Aitch would not be missed until knock-off time at the workshops, when security screws tallied all the movement-slips, workshop numbers, and sundry other things they did to keep tabs on everyone; and even after that, a search would be conducted for Aitch in the wrong place.

"Industrial workshops!" our escort screw called as he exited the medical centre to walk a dozen paces or so before again calling out. "Workshop men, line up on this man," indicating a prisoner he knew came up from the workshops.

Dale came and stood next to me, while I dawdled to allow a few to get into line ahead of us, before moving together into the ranks. The screw conducted a quick count . . . then a slower one . . . and declared that he was one short! "Industrial workshops!" he cried out, looking around for the missing inmate. He stared at his list of names. My mind raced. How could it be?

I felt a momentary surge of apprehension for Aitch and Dale – not for myself, I was in the clear and had no concerns – until Dale asked of me, wondering, "Is Bomber supposed to be with us?"

"Bomber is the one!" I spontaneously cried, using his nickname. I instantly corrected myself by blabbing his surname, reminding the screw, *ever so helpful*, by adding, "He's still inside on the gurney." To make it clear in his mind, I added, "The one who ate the roses." No way did I want a rollcall to happen.

The screw muttered angrily as he went back inside. Dale was visibly nervous; it was obvious he had not done this kind of thing before. I praised him, saying it took balls to risk the bashing he would get from security if caught. He became more agitated, so maybe I should have left that bit of knowledge unsaid. Just as well I refrained from mentioning the reception biff every inmate got when entering H-division; it may have toppled him over the edge.

Bomber arrived and fell into line at the rear. Dale told me he had two guys in his group who had promised to draw out their medical problem as long as they could, to give him more time to return. He had to get back before the count of his group, otherwise it would be him declared missing, and not Aitch! As we marched off, my nerves were on edge, still expecting a siren to wail its warning at any moment.

At the security box in industrial alley nothing untoward occurred. The count was correct and the escort screw returned the prisoners to their respective workshops. Not being in the tailor shop I missed out on seeing what went on when Dale stepped in there purporting to be Aitch. Nevertheless I found out later.

The moment he entered, two prisoners took him aside and sat him down where Aitch worked, while a third went straight to the overseer and complained of a migraine requesting that he be issued a movement-slip to get him to the infirmary, as soon as possible. This prisoner was known to have migraine issues and had made that request many times before. The overseer simply went ahead and wrote one out for him.

He walked confidently towards the gate as he signalled Dale to come to him. Dale stood there when he called over a different outside security screw to the one that had opened the gate earlier. By the time the screw arrived Dale had taken possession of the slip. With just a cursory look, the screw unlocked the gate and let him out. Dale headed for the security box, movement-slip clutched tight like a talisman and, as I imagine, chanting a mantra that everything would be all right.

Four hundred inmates worked daily in the industrial section.

Staff movements and relocation of prisoners occurred every day, so the odds of meeting a screw who knew both Dale and the migraine man were extremely unlikely. And so it was. They processed Dale without a glimmer of recognition, and off to the clinic he sped, to rejoin his group with ample time to spare, the bogus movement-slip torn up and binned the moment he reached there.

When the workday ended, each gang was assembled outside their shop where the men were counted by their overseer before marching down to be ticked off the book by security. After that, they were sent further along to be searched by a gauntlet of screws prior to being released to their divisions: normally a smooth and quick-run process. But this time, as we were marched down workshop alley towards the exit road, I could see ahead that something had gone wrong for them. The tailor-shop gang was clustered to the side of the security box, held back. They should have gone ahead of the wire-netting gang, who were always the last gang to leave.

While being counted, I listened to every snippet and gem of information thrown about. "Well I'm here, aren't I? I'm no figment!" protested a voice.

To which an angry screw replied, snapping, "But there's no movement-slip showing you returned!"

"I'm here, aren't I? It's not like I'm missing!" The migraine guy had it under control, and it even sounded like he was enjoying the situation.

As we formed a line up the slope to be searched, I heard a security screw conclude with one of his associates, "He has to be hiding in the tailor-shop, everything shows he returned here."

Not until two hour later did a report go public: prison authorities conceded defeat after two civilians on Champ Street separately reported that they had watched a person slide down a rope and stroll away. By then of course all the B–division inmates had been fed, showered, and locked away for the night. When I heard a roar of voices at five o'clock, and ribald comments shouted throughout the division, I knew Aitch had made the news (a convicted murderer had escaped from Pentridge) but I had no reason to listen to the radio. Tomorrow he would be front page in every state. How long he lasted out there did not really matter. Aitch had outwitted the system.

13
RAMBLE

The ballad of Reading Gaol

VILE DEEDS LIKE POISON WEEDS, BLOOM WELL IN PRISON AIR, IT IS ONLY WHAT IS GOOD IN MAN, THAT WASTES AND WITHERS THERE

- Oscar Wilde

In the 70s a meat pie cost $1, and a bottle of Heinz tomato sauce always sat on the counter ready for a generous dollop of free sauce for every customer. A grand-final ticket to the football for a family of four, plus a soft drink each, cost just $25. Boiled eggs in a bowl, cubes of cheese on a plate, with sliced bread were provided free as nibbles on the bar at any local pub. The largest denomination coin in circulation was $1, and 1c and 2c coins had value.

If something cost $100, it took at least two bank notes to pay for it — $100 notes were not printed until the 80s. A $5 note covered a four-pot shout at the bar, and readily available handguns could be purchased for as little as $350, with a box of bullets included. You could purchase a family car for $12,000 with a kid's seat thrown in if you wanted one. And a gallon of petrol (4.2 litres) cost $1.50. Every pavilion at the Melbourne Show handed out free show-bags, filled to the brim, overflowing with promotional give-a-ways, my favourite being tiny jars of Vegemite. A mesmerising variety of fireworks were available in suburban shops for Guy Fawkes Night (now forgotten) and after Christmas celebrations to welcome in the New Year, purchased over the counter legitimately by any kid who could make a decision and carried enough money to pay for them.

The contraceptive pill liberated married couples and helped young women overcome their sexual reticence. HIV had not yet emerged from continental Africa to become the scourge that hit the world for a six in the late 80s . . . again sending everyone back into a state of sexual repression.

A labourer's average wage of $118 per week bought more for a worker back then than the minimum wage of $460 an employee earns now. A room to rent for a week cost $25 with breakfast included, and a one bedroom flat like I had in Albert Park, two streets from the Esplanade and beach, cost $170 a month. But I refused to work back then: I thought slaving for a wage was a mug's game.

+ + + +

THE FIRST FATALITY, IN A SHOOTOUT, IS ACCURACY

The seventh decade of the twentieth century challenged established beliefs and awakened nascent minds to previously denied processes. Being in my prime years, I ignored society and went for it. Inevitably I ended up in prison three times. If only I had taken baby steps and experienced life around me, I may have appreciated my freedom more.

Every other day I would be out scouting in a 'worker' (a cheap second-hand car purchased under a false name, usually abandoned after a month of parking tickets that were never going to be paid, or burnt if involved in anything more serious) tailing armoured trucks delivering pay packets or, best of all, picking up cash. In the 70s, ATMs had not been invented; and there was no such thing as direct credit of wages into a bank account.

Hotels were always on my menu because of the money that continuously flowed over their counters, often secured in safes so antiquated that they must have been shipped over from England and Scotland with the First Fleet. One job a month always paid the rent, plus lots of extras! The most money I ever lifted was $68,000. Even now in the twenty-first century it still sounds like a tidy sum. But back then it was an absolute fortune (multiply it four times). Two travel bags were needed to tote the swag away. And buckets of coins too bulky to take had to be left behind.

It needed three of us to do the job. The safe that held the cash was secured inside an up-to-date strongroom which fought us every step of the way; being drill-proof and explosive-resistant, and *almost* cut-proof, it took three hours of non-stop assault before we could enter that room. I used malleable wire cut from an old farm fence, high in carbon, to feed under the intense heat of the cutting flame to break down the integrity of the one-inch (twenty-four millimetres) alloy-steel plate of the strongroom door: the principle underlying a modern oxy-acetylene powder-set using aluminium powder and iron oxide. It took another two hours of stress and toil to open the double-door safe inside. Thankfully it was an old Chubb. Two of us worked side by side while the third kept nit on the roof of a council building two streets away. Using a Bearcat scanner (state-of-the-art direct from America) to eavesdrop on police frequencies and watchmen patrolling in the area, we were continually updated by our nit-keeper via two-way.

The take-home was $21,000 each. The discrepancy of $5,000 went my way, off the top first. I got the extra because I took the gamble of putting up the original seed-cash needed to buy all the equipment to guarantee success, and most importantly, an untraceable, reliable van. (Shonky car-yard salesmen constantly duped buyers until the 80s when roadworthy certificates became mandatory with the sale of any registered vehicle.)

Twenty-one grand back in the 70s is equivalent to eighty thousand-plus now. If only I had stopped! Aged twenty-four I owned a house in South Melbourne, had three growing bank accounts, and drove a good set of wheels . . . but a fine line exists between need and greed. And like a lot of criminals, my eyes were bigger than my belly: I grew overly greedy.

Prison became an unwanted place for me to be in during the 70s. Most of my prime years were wasted. Severely curtailed to an existence of austerity, pain, isolation, and forced introspection, I missed out on partying, screwing hippy chicks, working for a wage, and summer holidays. I never had a normal start to life, but that was my choice.

I enjoyed the argy-bargy of violence in the criminal milieu (but was never violent towards honest citizens) and as a consequence always carried a weapon of one kind or another which I willingly used when offended or set upon. I participated in numerous carefully planned crimes for large sums of money, but then quite often I contradicted that logic by wittingly committing gratuitous offences for no gain at all other than the sheer hubris of committing them! In one such example of folly which went dramatically wrong, I copped two bullets in the head in a shoot-out with police.

Some of my astute associates suggested it may have been my salvation when the court sentenced me to a long term of servitude for that stupid offence. Sure, I went on to commit further offences after being released in the late 70s, but I could have died in that shoot-out with two to the head, don't you think? I know of a few who are no longer with us who died from just one piece of lead better placed, so I gave their observations due thought.

Being slammed up forced me to acknowledge my confrontational nature and recognise that I had almost gone rogue like a bull elephant expelled from the herd. That harsh recognition learnt in the educational, ever challenging cauldron of prison strife allowed me to step back from a precipice which I might not have seen if left to my own resources on the streets of Melbourne. In suburbia a weak criminal can flee when violence escalates and becomes a bit too hot to handle and never be forced to confront a cowardly inner self, but in prison you cannot run away and hide when trouble brews: in prison, there is nowhere to run! You *must* step up.

A few guys I grew up with did not make it past the 80s. They are long dead because of disputes and the life-style we led, while I survived in prison. Because of that, should I thank the heartless judge for incarcerating me at such a critical period in my life, and shake the hands of the two arseholes that shot me down? Not likely! I hope they have all suffered for their abuse of power when they dealt unjustly with me. So who really knows how it would have turned out for me? The past cannot be changed, so I let it go and moved on. I have no room for regrets. I'm still alive and experiencing a good life.

And as a postscript, I can sincerely say that I gave self-analysis my best shot. It eventually worked out all right for me considering the crap espoused in prison and perpetrated by those better positioned and better informed than me when it came to rehabilitation. A callous, vindictive system withheld all help when I most needed it.

+ + + +

AN ACCIDENT INVESTIGATION OFFICER FOR A VEHICLE INSURANCE COMPANY ASKED THE YOUNG FEMALE DRIVER, "WHAT GEAR WERE YOU IN WHEN THE ACCIDENT HAPPENED?" AND SHE ARTLESSLY REPLIED, "A SILK BLOUSE, JEANS, AND REEBOK SNEAKERS."

- Unknown

During the seventh decade of the twentieth century when all nine planets in our solar system were lined up, the values and social restraints of the earlier periods in Australia were more forcefully challenged than they had ever previously been. Social change occurred throughout Australia, whether or not you participated. Authority and positions of influence in the 70s were taken for granted as a God-given right, and discrimination between race, sex, religion, and social classes was actively practised, making it a bloody battleground of grievances as awareness of inequality and injustices grew and bloomed. In addition to forging social changes for the betterment of society, every Australian state experienced riotous behaviour and disobedience within their prison system and underwent major law reform. In prison, being caught up in that eventful decade of turmoil adversely changed my attitude towards society. A consequence of those dynamic Aquarius years were spent by me in prison along with other likeminded prisoners fighting for rights which should already have been ours, enshrined in law. But by doing so, our activities were labelled criminal and harsh punishments were common. But without that incarceration and bloody struggle decades ago, I would never have grown into the person I now feel comfortable and confident being.

The majority of those who end up in prison feel victimised, unfairly dealt with by the police and courts, like being marooned on a leaky ship mid-ocean against their will, pleading for the vessel to dock before it sinks and drowns them, unable to improve themselves by utilising the time productively and learning from the journey and the events around them.

A prison is not a place of punitive confinement if you are able to transform the shift of location to one of the physical body only. Unfettered mentally, the mind will soar free. After accomplishing that state of mind, it is easier to accept the prison reality as an experiential journey and let the sentence get on with itself. In the end, basically, that is how I did my time.

+ + + +

THE GREATER THE POWER, THE MORE DANGEROUS THE ABUSE

- Edmund Burke

My mother was an avid card-player as well as a heavy smoker. The cards kept her smart, the cigarettes eventually killed her. Everyone just lit up with ashtrays built into the arm-rests of the chairs we sat on, and it was the non-smoker who sneaked out for a reviver of fresh air! It was not obligatory to go outside for a smoke in her day. Why passive smoking has never taken me out with cancer is probably because a bullet is still waiting for me somewhere out there.

After a massive stroke which paralysed her right side, mum belatedly swore off cancer-sticks. Organising evening card games, usually hold-'em poker, became my mum's remaining vice, and she would bet big: as many as fifty matchsticks (5c per match) would be slammed on the table daring an opponent to take her on! She out-bluffed me many times.

In the big picture of risk including unprotected sex, speeding, and alcohol abuse, to mention a few minor ones to put it in perspective, loss of money sits in a similar scale on the lower end of gambling. Consequently, some gamblers need to experience higher risk to get their kicks and quickly progress to the next level of addiction on the wheel of chance: extreme sport and dangerous ventures. And within that group's mentality is a veiled underbelly to gambling where a small percent of the hard-core will unconsciously enter a progressively higher deadly level until finally their 'life' is wagered on top of everything else they risk.

With open arms, I would have welcomed my mum's steady head into our gang. If only I had stayed at the humdrum level of gambling with money, instead of stepping in to the heady, perilous field of crime. Of course the downside when gambling with your freedom is pain, humiliating capture, a trial and all the ignominy that entails, plus a term of imprisonment where body searches and anal probes are conducted every day − all beyond your control. Each day endured in prison, elements of pain wait around a corner out of sight ready to strike.

✛ ✛ ✛ ✛

YOU CANNOT AFFORD TO DIG YOUR HEELS IN WHEN YOU ARE HANGING BY YOUR FINGERTIPS

− Joe Tog

Collins English Dictionary definition for *Gamble*:

1. Plays a game of chance. 2. To risk, or bet (money, etc.) on the outcome of an event. 5. A risky act or venture. 6. A bet, wager, or

other risk taken for monetary gain – conduct a risky undertaking.

++++

During the first half of my life a risk-taking gene in human genomes, rarely acknowledged in society, repeatedly put me in peril! The thrill from gambling with money eventually waned and new ways to stimulate were sought. I risked more and more until unwittingly, I gambled my freedom daily and even my life! And I paid a heavy price for not being able to recognise my problem as an advanced form of gambling, until ending in prison a third time! My problem was that I enjoyed too much the adrenalin rush that came with taking risk and not always of the conventional variety.

In the hurly-burly of getting through each day, we are called upon to constantly make decisions, and most of us succeed at doing that, though very few are able to recognise it as a form of gambling because of the muddle between the decision to perform an action and its outcome. Unfortunately that daily buzz is not enough for a small percent of seriously afflicted gamblers. As contrary as it is, human nature struggled through thousands of generations spent surviving the perilous nomadic hunter-gatherer's existence to become the safer law-abiding society we now are. An everyday risk becomes boring, so individuals with a strong hunter gene seek greater excitement at a higher level. Casino operators exploit that weakness to the full.

By trying as hard as we can, all of us strive to bring order to our lives believing the decisions we make are routine and not risks, and therefore normal. The educated punters (read that as stock-brokers) think they are above it all and in control when making financial decisions, but they are no different to the hunter stalking a meal in the bush: only the method and place has changed.

My personal observation is that country people seem to frequent gambling venues less than the city slickers. Perhaps their gambling gene is put at ease by the many decisions they are forced to make when sowing a crop, trying to forecast the weather months ahead, or when lambing season is underway with foxes on the prowl, and knowing sale prices will be subject to international market fluctuations not in their control.

But for those leading a mundane or orderly lifestyle, where excitement has fled the scene and life has become monotonous (welcome to my world) a casino with all of its flashing lights and glitzy hype beckons as an exciting venue for a night out. Beginner's luck netting that first big win (a huge incentive to keep going) is what sucks in and cements a punter's mind. From that moment on, the belief begins that luck is predictable. The dicey road a gambler follows, in whatever form, is paved with tales of woe and loss.

I only wager money now, unlike when younger and I regrettably squandered my youthful years. Crime is an under-the-radar form of gambling, and is seriously addictive, as insidious and destructive as chemical drugs. It hooked me in and warped my life. Be very, *very sure*, that the same detrimental gene is not interfering with the quality of your life.

+ + + +

CORRELATION IS NOT CAUSATION

- Joe Tog

In the hand of an aggressive carpenter a hammer mutates into a weapon when wielded with malice. Yet in the hands of a farmer concerned about the safety of his newborn lambs a rifle is not a weapon when used to protect them from fox predation, no different in kind than if a trap had been used instead.

Under the Regulated Weapons Act (in Victorian law) any tool, device, or other thing used aggressively becomes in law a weapon. A tool of any kind remains a tool until its function is abused. A firearm in the military is already defined as a weapon because of its intended use to kill humans, whereas a firearm in the hands of a civilian is not *ipso facto* a weapon, even though it is universally perceived as such by police.

A biro becomes a weapon if poked in an eye, but only if it has been done intentionally. The 410 shotgun my partner owns is not a weapon when its sole purpose is to shoot destructive rabbits that plague our veggie garden. Also, any type of firearm used for humane purposes such as a veterinarian would use to dispatch a suffering or critically injured animal cannot possibly be viewed as a weapon. Its single function is to relieve an animal from suffering, not inflict it.

Consider a hypodermic needle at inoculation time, when the pain that hurts them causes young children to cry. No one in their right mind would consider a needle as being in a catalogue of weapons. Yet in a street robbery, when a druggie experiencing withdrawal menaces a victim with a used hypodermic, it must be just as frightening as though a pistol was poked in their face. It *then* becomes a weapon.

It is not what a tool is, but how that tool is misused that defines it as a weapon. So when I hear police constantly refer to firearms in homes as weapons – firearms intended solely for a shooting range and NOT for criminal use – I shake my head in bewilderment. What can they possibly be thinking? If their common sense is so skewed about firearms, where else are they in error when it comes to enforcement? Correct interpretation of a potentially harmless situation is everything, and when they get that wrong, as they often do when personalities come in conflict with the law, reading more into a situation can lead to abuse of power.

Many years ago, when intercepted by two undercover detectives and my car searched, a baseball bat was discovered on the back seat. They perceived it as a weapon and questioned me over it. My indignant response and criticism of their intelligence – I asserted that the ball had been lost, and did not own a glove – culminated in my being arrested on a trumped-up charge. Their skewed mentality identified it as a weapon, whereas I used it as a piece of sport equipment.

If I had really desired to pack a weapon that day, a long-handled quarter-axe or a bull-prod would have been my preferred choice. I have utilised both and been *very* satisfied with the outcome, especially the prod. And of course neither of those tools were weapons until I misused them as such.

Suspicion becomes paranoia, when the facts are cloaked by fear. In skilled hands a nail-file *could* become a weapon, but in the hands of an incompetent a nail-file is still a nail-file no matter what the intention. A bikie pulled from the shower and arrested by police (yes, most of them do wash) would seemingly not pose much of a threat standing there naked, but compared to a dopey squarehead running amok with a knife, the bikie's fists would be far more dangerous. Yet time after time rattled police have shot recklessly when they would have been better served if they had stayed calm and not become overwhelmed by the fear of a minor knife threat.

A pistol pointed with menace at someone to subdue their intention is a weapon – deadly weapon, in fact. Yet what good is a deadly weapon to the police if the offender is so affected by drugs or delusional that they are incapable of cognitively comprehending that threat? And a firearm is absolutely useless if the threat of being shot is ignored, or not believed. A competently wielded baton, and mace judiciously sprayed with a bit of shock therapy thrown in, would be far more effective.

+ + + +

80/20 PRINCIPLE

Roughly 80% of work will be done by 20% of the workers. In most societies, 20% of motorists cause 80% of road accidents. 20% of beer drinkers consume 80% of all beer. And finally, 20% of criminals commit 80% of all crimes.

+ + + +

When pressed to give an honest answer, every friend I have, *without exception*, has admitted to gambling in one form or another at some time in their life. Some confessed to the thrill of getting away with stealing a few things or having smuggled something trivial into the country, but in the telling, each tried to justify their actions. Financial pressure, a moment of weakness, and outright greed were three of the reasons given. From that limited anecdotal knowledge I am forced to conclude (right or wrong) that *everyone* has a touch of the pirate in them. To add to the accretion of proof, the most watched videos after X-rated are crime-based.

Taking risk is an inherent survival trait in all mammals, but ownership is not. Laws covering theft of someone else's possessions are man-made to protect the owner. Humans practise the Rule of Law when it comes to ownership: no other animal does it. 'Right by might' prevails throughout the world in the animal kingdom. I am not complaining, just pointing out an overlooked fact that most citizens are programmed early and appropriately as children to coexist harmoniously in society, but as life flows on there are always those few who missed the school bus from time to time, through no fault of their own, and consequently, because of that imperfect conditioning, walk on the wild side of life.

What possible cause would induce a person to smuggle drugs on or, even worse, inside their body unless it is greed combined with stupidity? The greedy bit I can understand because I've been there, but the stupid aspect is inexcusable. A degree in rocket science is not required to carry out research in a library or peruse newspaper archives. If something needs to be built – and I am not suggesting a house here – the very least one should do is draw up a simple plan and then experiment a bit with the tools available to be sure the job can be successfully completed. Otherwise by winging it, failure is almost a certainty. Yet we constantly hear of smugglers being intercepted in airport terminals simply because *they* thought they were clever, and smarter than everyone else. Customs must shake their collective heads in bewilderment and delight each time they take into custody a clever-dick smuggler who thinks they have invented a foolproof smuggling method.

When the actor Yul Brunner found out he was dying of lung cancer, he became desperate to get the message out there in an anti-smoking commercial: *Just don't smoke. The smoking of one cigarette can mutate a lung-cell and turn it cancerous.* He meant the very first cigarette could be the one that triggers the mutation. Yet so many smokers believe cancer is caused by the *quantity* of cigarettes smoked per day, and so they continue to gamble with their health by smoking less. Smugglers must rationalise their conduct in a similar way. In the pain-and-grief world of petty smugglers the wheel is reinvented every day. It is bewildering why they do it.

At least a hundred different ways to smuggle articles into Australia have been told to me over the decades and not just drugs. Some of them were clever in their simplicity, and others were extremely complex; yet all are known to customs, so unless a unique way can be devised, all new methods are just old methods with a modern tweak to them. Why would any rational person take the risk of smuggling, knowing that success hinged on being shielded from arrest by an imaginary entity called Lady Luck, unless they actually believed in her?

Greed and need are two primary motivators, but the gamblers' urge underlying the belief that the system can be controlled is what allows it to occur. I've tried smuggling and failed, while others I know have had resounding success, yet when objectively assessed it could just as easily have gone the other way. A sweaty brow detected in the airport terminal, or a nervous tic when loading a container at the ship yard, or missing a warning phone call from an accomplice, could be the simple difference between arrest and pulling it off. Customs performance is measured by success but a drug smuggler *cannot afford to fail once*! If contraband is located in someone's possession, investigation and enforcement follows, then prison is likely for those involved. Yet, still they do it. Confiscated goods are similar to chips forfeited on a roulette wheel, or a hunting spear broken on rocks when it misses its target. Gambling in diverse ways has gone on since humans roamed the globe in search of food.

My theory is that gambling and criminality are, in some ways, synonymous. Just the terms of reference differ. I once watched two crims in prison fight each other to a standstill over a bet that one was a better boxer than the other. Both lost when exhaustion forced them to stop, and then the screws who watched the fight from behind the protection of a locked gate entered and handcuffed both and marched them off to the punishment division. It would be harder now in a more liberal prison system to confidently define an act of gambling around my model, but when I served time in Pentridge through the 70s an austere environment existed where very few prison perks existed. Gambling was one of the solid threads that connected *every* inmate throughout the network.

Selfish prisoners have stabbed those they owed a debt to, rather than pay. And of course as a matter of principle, others have bashed those who welshed on a bet. I know prisoners who embraced gambling to escape reality, but when the consequences caught up with them and their life was threatened for non payment, they fled to authority and begged for protection but that always came at a price. Some in pure desperation have been drawn in so deep that they committed outrageous crimes to get out from under debt, to avoid injury or death themselves. It all eventually becomes an ocean of grey as emotions merge with each other and the gambling aspect is submerged beneath the pressure of survival.

Because the itch to gamble is buried so deeply in our psyche, it bubbles out in the most unlikely ways. An honest law-abiding citizen, properly programmed, will shoplift a can of tuna without knowing the underlying reasons of why, and then traumatise over the shame of it when they are caught. A High Court judge took a calculated gamble when he swore on oath in a Sydney courtroom, saying someone else drove his car when questioned over a traffic offence, later proven that he deliberately lied to conceal his guilt. An owner-trainer gambled on not being suspected when he doped his own horse – the odds-on favourite in the race – to *lose* so that he could bet on the second favourite in the same race with triple the odds. And jockeys are renowned for gambling on horses tipped to win that they are not riding, often in the same race!

Anyone who enjoys jumping out of a plane at two thousand metres with a flimsy silk parachute on their back is a personified gambler beyond dispute. If that chute fails to deploy correctly, death is inevitable. That calculated danger – flirting with death – is what gives such an adrenalin rush each time they jump. Losing *everything* on one gamble often gives a better rush than an actual win. Ask any devotee of the roulette wheel. Or talk to the bank teller I met in prison, who rushed out of the bank at lunchtime with a customer's deposit to bet on a certainty he heard of in the third race. Overlaying that reckless gambling action was a serious criminal act only vaguely considered until the horse came in fourth, and by then it was too late for the teller to curb the urge.

I am not referring to habituated criminal activities that through daily repetition blur and become blasé. If a skydiver jumped out of a plane every morning, it too would lose its stimulation and become the same as driving city traffic each day. The possibility of death or serious injury is forever there, yet commuters who forget it continue to gamble and die on the road daily because the risk fades through familiarity. Without a gambling urge very few of us would venture out and blithely negotiate the dangerous traffic situations that exist.

Every time a thief climbs through a broken window or on to a steeply gabled roof, a gamble is taking place. Not just the risk of being cut by glass or falling to the ground, but a far deeper one of facing imprisonment if caught. It took me years to comprehend that the atavistic urge came from a deeply buried primitive zone of our brain. Adapt or die – by taking acceptable risk to stave off failure – is a natural fundamental of life.

Setting fire to a house riddled with white ants is a gamble taken by the arsonist owner in isolation, not knowing that every insurance company is alert to that scam. Heavily insure a racehorse that can never be a champion, then claim for the insurance after a callous scoundrel shoots it; no different than the hundreds of vehicles that are burned every year by their owners to falsely claim insurance. A cleanskin criminal (unconvicted) buys a stolen plasma television from a petty thief for the house – a reasonable gamble of not being caught, every house has a television – not suspecting for a moment that it will be re-stolen a week later and sold on. Who will they report the theft to?

I heard recently of a French mantle clock being sold very cheaply at $2000 to a greedy businessman. It had a digital camera/recorder expertly fitted inside, with a wireless transmitter for downloading. The information the perpetrator gained over the next two weeks concerning a land development scheme returned him fifty times the real cost of the clock.

In earlier decades, police and other enforcement agencies were able to access and use expensive and hard-to-acquire technology to stay ahead of criminals, but advanced technology is now cheap and readily available to every strata of society through the internet. And the myriad ways telephonic technology is being abused staggers belief. Tiny tracking devices woven into the packaging of a parcel, not the content, are commonly used now by both sides of the law.

Identity theft is a burgeoning type of crime that once was barely worth the effort; it now earns millions of dollars from those who want the guise of an Australian identity. Every year a score or so of needy cleanskins sell their own identities, like people who sell a kidney or an eye. Only this way is better for them; they get to keep what they sell. And instead of a counterfeit passport only good to defraud a business, it becomes a cloned identity used to board an overseas flight and travel incognito to any country in the world.

14
WASTED EFFORT

A typical prison knife

TO TRIUMPH ONE MUST FIRST DARE

- Joe Tog

Locked away in my cell for the night, I sat on the end of the bed staring at shadows on the bluestone wall cast by the security lights outside. I sifted mentally through what had been proposed by a fellow inmate, who believed he had found a way to guarantee an escape plan I had discussed in theory, not really believing it could be done but idly considered to pass the time. Pentridge prison confined a fluctuating population of eleven hundred prisoners or so, and every day somewhere in the prison an escape plot was being hatched. Probably thousands have conspired through the years believing they could do it, to kill time. Scores have tried and failed, but only a few handful were left who actually had the ability and balls to successfully engineer an escape from a maximum security prison.

There are no new ways to escape from a prison; down through prison history *every* conceivable escape plan has been tried before. A new way is an old one with a modern tweak to suit the situation, so the idea of taking a hostage to break out of prison was nothing new. Historically, since convict days it has been tried a score of times with variations in many prisons across Australia, and in response to that a number of seasoned protocols by authorities were well and truly in place. The key response by prison staff in a hostage situation is delaying tactics, slowing it down to allow a hostage recovery plan to get underway, whilst appearing to give the hostage-taker demands consideration. All of that takes time and, if managed deceptively and full advantage taken by us, would give the strategic twist in this plan the potential to work. It played into the hands and minds of what prison security expected: crude violence rather than clever artifice.

The proposal behind the plan which had me believing it could work was two-pronged: one involving a hostage to deliberately grab the full attention of a tower guard, while a covert plan ran parallel with a good chance of success even without the first one to draw attention away from the real strategy. When combined, they appeared unbeatable.

B-division was a two-storey building in the shape of a Christian cross filled with serious, bad-arsed offenders, built in 1859 when consideration for the inmates' comfort was not on the agenda. With every window heavily barred and only three exit gates, each within close shooting range of an armed guard in a tower, to contemplate escape while being used as target practice was a difficult task. Two exercise yards with unrestricted access existed for the recreation of all B-division inmates, built between two wings of the division, opposite sides of the main wing. A decade earlier, yard-one had been used to launch a bold attack on the tower which overlooked it, when Ronald Ryan and Peter Walker escaped in 1963, unfortunately culminating in a warden being shot dead outside the prison. Ronald Ryan was later convicted and hung for murder. (In the light of new evidence the controversy over whether he, or a guard in another tower, actually fired the fatal shot has never been satisfactorily settled.)

That tower straddled the junction of two walls and controlled a small gate below it. While the sentry above was distracted pulling a lever to unlock the gate in the perimeter wall to admit a warden returning from lunch, Ryan and Walker placed a makeshift ladder made out of timbers removed from a rain-shelter in the centre of the yard, assembled when the yard screw was distracted by a gabby accomplice, and quickly ascended it. Months of secret manoeuvrings had gone into its construction. Up the ladder they both scrambled and across to the walkway attached to the tower to grapple the rifle from the surprised tower guard ... and history followed. That tower immediately had the best security upgrade of all the towers within Pentridge.

The far wall of yard-two was noticeably different. Unlike yard-one which had two bluestone walls of equal height to complete the square, yard-two had a blank wall of bluestone which rose so high that it matched the two-storey wall of B-division. The view from the tower originally constructed there to oversee yard-two was blocked by that wall which was one side of a large building used to make coir mats, built onto the end of the divisional wing fifty years after the prison's completion, contrary to the original prison design. The guard in that tower only saw yard-two inmates when he advanced more than twenty-five paces from the actual corner tower to the end of an extended walkway atop the outside wall.

At a right angle similar to the first walkway on top of a joining perimeter wall, a second walkway (this one was of standard length) overlooked a narrow waste area of land, and the locked side-gate of the coir workshop. Outside the prison wall a pedestrian footpath meandered all the way to the busy Sydney Road and Bell Street corner.

By working out angles I knew that when the guard stood at the end of the extended walkway to look into yard-two, the other walkway (and most importantly the tower door onto it) could not be seen by the guard. This was the Achilles heel of Pentridge, overlooked by prison security for decades, a weak point making the escape plan doable. That security defect finally swayed me.

+ + + +

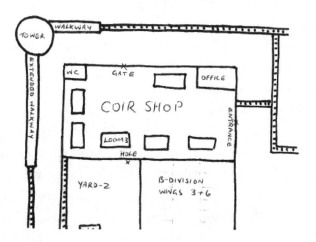

An average of twenty-four inmates were assigned to the coir-shop, all classified as 'intractable' and not expected to work; though on the prison books appearing to be gainfully employed.

Instead of gambling with cards, bullshitting to each other, and playing board games as usual, now that escape was a possibility, we conspired and talked about the prospect of freedom each and every day. The building we did this from was long and narrow with the entrance at the front controlled by a lazy overseer who rarely left his office, waiting for retirement; with an internal guard (sometimes two) whose sole duty was to perambulate the shop and give the impression of being alert, but instructed to basically do nothing that might disturb the 'harmony' of the place. They were rotated fortnightly, always under the pump of not knowing whether they would be assaulted or not. An air of physical menace pervaded the shop, intimidating to anyone unfamiliar with that kind of testosterone environment. The constant turnover of screws meant they never fully grasped the goings-on in the shop. And all of that meshed in nicely as part of our plan.

Six cumbersome timber-constructed nineteenth century coir looms, no longer operational, enveloped in dusty spider webs, were spaced evenly around the shop floor. Decommissioned a decade before, the three largest of them lined a windowless wall (the other side was B-division's yard-two), while the wall opposite with four barred windows and a chained gate allowed sunlight to stream through and light the area. There was no back door. The circular guard tower, mounted where two walls met eight metres from the building's corner, cast an oppressive presence over the coir shop: a continual reminder of our imprisonment. Like the mythical sword of Damocles (only this one was real), it hovered over our heads every day.

Traditionally, a card game called red-aces (preferred by inmates throughout the prison) was played seemingly without end within the gutted frame of loom three, a partly dismantled loom with only its outer bulky timbers still standing. Blankets hanging over the top and down each side gave the players partial privacy from the rest of the noisy workshop population. With only minor adjustments and some vocal argument to dissuade the shop screws from pursuing the purpose of an extra blanket being introduced, one was hung from the back of the loom to make the gambling den appear a little cosier. (It also conveniently concealed the wall from the sight of any screw passing by and peering in.)

Within a fortnight the blanket had become part of the accepted décor like the other three, no longer pulled down during random workshop searches for contraband carried out by security screws after prisoners had left and been locked up for the night. Up to this stage of the escape plan nothing had actually occurred that could warrant an internal charge, and only four people knew exactly what was going on: myself, my friend John who tweaked the plan, and two armed robbers. We thought it best that the assault on the tower be done by those experienced in that field and confident with a gun. But the problem for us now was that others were becoming aware that something out of the ordinary was astir.

The dynamics within the workplace were very volatile, even hostile most times, such that even the slightest variance in one's habit triggered alarm bells in paranoid minds. To calm the spectre of a violent outburst by a susceptible inmate – after all, we *had* spent a few days covertly inspecting timbers in all the looms to calculate if there was enough small pieces available to build a six metre ladder to reach the tower walkway – our intentions were therefore broached to a few we trusted implicitly, knowing they would dampen any wrongly developing suspicions heard. But each one we told immediately wanted to be included in the escape!

On the day chosen to go, those involved had blown out to an incredible fourteen: eleven men in the coir shop had become active participants, plus three lifers from within the division … but I'm getting ahead of how it unfolded. The planning part of any escape is easy; it carries no risk. Implementing it, though, is drawn-out and nerve-racking, in constant risk of failure, apprehension and pain. But when it comes to the actual escape, the life-threatening act is mentally daunting to launch a surprise escalade on the tower guard. And it can be taken as a given, it never gets easier. I should know; I've successfully escaped from custody five times.

The original metal bolts and nuts used to join the jarrah timbers of the looms had rusted solid as though welded, and even if a spanner was 'borrowed' from the engineer's shop and smuggled to us, it would have been useless up against such accretion and multiple layers of paint. A solution was needed, and luckily we had one ready to hand, as used in the Ryan and Walker escape from yard-one. A few short lengths of galvanised water pipe, which once serviced a missing faucet, were still attached in places to the inside wall of the building. Two of those lengths soon went missing, but not before they could be replaced with lengths of dowel which looked uncannily like the original missing pieces. Potentially, we now had two hand-driven core drills, to fit over the bolt heads, to cut the wood.

With lots of notches cut in one end of the pipe (by slamming it repeatedly into the sharp edge of a steel bracket when the shop radio blared out a race-call) and the other end wrapped with rag to protect my hand from injury, a repetitive to-and-fro circular action with a bit of pressure applied soon proved to our satisfaction that the experiment worked, confirming the makings of a ladder could begin. Throughout the rest of that day, only stopping when warned by the radio station being adjusted that one of the screws was on the move, the sharp metal teeth of the pipe steadily cut their way deeper and deeper into a wooden strut, circling the bolt until the wooden cross member attached to it was reached. The first rung of a not yet existent ladder had been successfully acquired – only fourteen more rungs to go.

Behind the extra blanket hanging in the card-players' loom, movements were occurring, probably suspected as homosexual activities by those few men not in the know; but the cause of the movements was not as crass as that. A bluestone block in the wall of the coir shop had been carefully selected for removal by locating where a prisoner tapped with an aluminium mug in yard-two to the rhythmical beat of a song played on the divisional speaker. That block behind loom three exactly matched the *only* brick in yard-two that could conceivably be worked on and removed in relative secrecy.

Square in shape, hewn a hundred years earlier by toiling convicts in the prison quarry, a measuring mistake in the block's manufacture had made it a centimetre thinner than it should have been, and rather than be set aside and not used by the stonemason it had been deliberately placed low, three courses up from the ground, when the building was being built. It required a double thickness of mortar between it and the two blocks it sat on below to bring it up level for the next course. The perspective made the imperfection impossible to see by a person standing, virtually undetectable except for the fact that long before my time an enterprising convict had spotted the flaw and capitalised its potential to his own use. That extra thickness of mortar when removed left a gap of two centimetres under the entire bluestone block, a space successfully utilised for decades, passed down from 'owner to owner' with all kinds of contraband successfully stored there.

By first using one-penny nails salvaged from the looms and then long bolts as they were acquired, the crumbly mortar securing a bluestone block in the workshop slowly disappeared, worn away by constant abrasion. And each afternoon the mortar dust was mixed with bread and water to make a paste, and pushed back into the course as filler to foil detection if a search of that area occurred. With only a few anxious hiccups along the way, work on removing the block steadily progressed.

By the second week of serious assault on the wall it was thought by all of us that everyone else in the shop basically knew what was going on, except the screws (and how they missed it is beyond me) as mistakes and near misses occurred almost daily. The worst time was when the 'tools' were not hidden away and left lying in sight overnight, undetected on the red-brick floor until picked up and pocketed next morning by the overseer's gofer (distrusted simply because he did the bookwork for the overseer and came from E-division), who by sheer chance had preceded the overseer's ritual morning tour of the workshop before he allowed any prisoners to enter. The first I knew that the gofer was aware of our escape plan was when he slipped me the 'forgotten' tools. All night I had worried, and it was such a relief to learn why we weren't being frogmarched to H-division that I spontaneously offered him a position in the escape. He declined the offer, but said he was willing to help, so I spread the word that he was with us. After that the crew invited him to play cards and he became a regular habitué of loom three.

Our greatest worry was that a turncoat might bargain his way out of the coir shop, maybe even the prison, by informing. To foil the mass escape of so many hardened criminals would be an incredible coup for any screw, and the gofer could have done it without any of us being the wiser. But no one ever did inform, and I believe it was because we made everyone feel part of it by putting our trust in them.

To introduce an odd fact only crims seem to know, when the word *informer* is used in a criminal milieu it is intended as an intensely pejorative word, not the way police use it to label an *informant* who is simply doing what any normal law-abiding citizen should do when assisting police in a criminal investigation.

A disgruntled associate of a criminal who discloses secret knowledge to police (or more cunningly, leaks it to a weaker person they know will pass it on) is an informer, and usually benefits the turncoat to the harm of those squealed on. (Any information of value to police or a court is invariably of criminal content which *will* put someone in deep shit.) This treacherous Judas (to label them a 'dog' is to insult the canine family) collects a few 'pieces of silver' as reward for the back-stabbing deed.

As a general statement all prisoners classified to serve their time in B-division were there because they were hardened inmates and therefore the toughest in Pentridge – that definition covered petty thieves and recidivists up to organised career criminals and murderers – who obeyed the rules of the division, no different from inmates in other divisions, to earn monthly remission and to guarantee fortnightly visits from their wives and children, etcetera. So when I say the worst in B-division worked in the coir workshop, I'm not suggesting they were all hardnosed criminals; far from it. The coir shop was the last resort by the authorities to control and segregate 'troublemakers' in B-division who deliberately challenged the right of the prison governor to enforce outdated prison rules. An example of a few 'crimes' that put me in B-division's coir-shop were that I refused to shave (a prison offence), refused to work (a prison offence), challenged every order given (a prison offence), and when a screw struck me with his baton for a minor defiance, I took it from him and hurled it over the perimeter wall onto Champ Street at the front of the prison. But the most heinous offence I committed of all was to tell the governor of Pentridge in unambiguous language what he could do with his remission incentives (also a prison offence). All of those in the coir-shop had done something similarly defiant within the system, which bound us together in our differences; a kind of brotherhood even though many of us came from socially different backgrounds.

The development of the escape grew substantially as each step drew closer to reality: and of course the frayed nerves of everyone caused fallouts and dispute. Entering the third week, there had been two minor stabbings in the division and a half-dozen fights involving queue jumpers who thought, because they had been bullies on the streets standing over scared victims, they could continue their standover tactics inside; but they were promptly educated to the real reality that exists amidst men who are mentally tough, and not just physical wannabes. It had reached a flashpoint of no return.

The first ten days of sedulous work put in on the bluestone block in the coir-shop had ended in failure to remove it from the wall. By the seventh day of work on it all of the mortar had successfully been scraped away, but still it could not be removed; only a centimetre of movement was gained either way when using a long bolt in the groove to lever it. The last three days were spent worrying the problem mentally, while continuing with the ladder project. I finally learnt the solution to the masonry problem in an unrelated conversation about handguns and why they kicked so much when fired.

A bullet speeds to its target, propelled by incredible force generated by a tiny amount of ignited propellant expanding behind it in a closed chamber. And because the mini-explosion cannot burst the arsenal-grade steel of the barrel, it forces the bullet ahead of it at incredible speed towards the muzzle, while simultaneously punching the gun back at the hand that holds it. A way to crack the rock had been found. All that was needed now was some gunpowder, and I had a friend in prison who knew how to make it.

A year prior, an inmate had stopped me at the top of the stairs when about to descend and take a shower (the underground dungeons from an earlier prison era were renovated, converted to a shower-block, gym, and storage area) and he advised me not to go down and to stay away from there. Ignoring his advice, I went to step past him but he instantly blocked my passage with his arm which would normally have riled me somewhat, but I sensed something greater was underway.

I gave him a hard look and snarled, "I'll be back in ten minutes." He shrugged his shoulders as I walked off, and said, "See you then."

Sitting on the bed in my cell, trying to figure out why a crim guarded the stairs, I heard an almighty THUMP and a tremor shook the division. Out of the cell I ran because I knew it had something to do with the shower-block! Crims popped out of doorways everywhere. Some of them with a towel over their shoulder or in their hand obviously stopped from showering but still waiting just like me. I ran towards the stairs, passing by the three divisional prison guards standing silent, bewildered by the sudden explosion so close to their desk. The only person apparently not stopped going down to the dungeon area by the 'sentry' now bounded up the stairs towards me followed by a rising fog of fine grey dust and black smoke, blood spurting from the stumps of fingers on one hand while swiping blood from deep lacerations on his face with the other.

A screw blew alarm blasts of sound on his brass whistle, while the other two sprang into action and hurriedly unlocked the wing gate and held it open for the staggering victim to exit. From the sidelines the guy who had stopped my descent to the showers gave me a knowing nod as he strolled away. The smell of 'burnt metal' and ancient dust disturbed by the explosion (and whatever else lurked down there) deterred everyone from venturing into the unknown. No one took a shower that night.

When the bomb incident in B-division was still an ongoing

investigation by frustrated security (apparently no one saw or heard anything) I sat regularly with my friend and discussed everything *except* how the bomb was manufactured. It was not until a few months later that I learnt the cause of *why* it had happened, at the time having no interest in knowing how it was done. I now needed to learn the *how*.

That evening, locked in my cell for the night, I followed instructions carefully committed to memory on how to crush eighty match-heads along with a small piece of artist charcoal in an improvised mortar (my aluminium cup) and mix in a few drops of water to make enough fine paste to eventually fill a twist of paper the size of a cigarette. The primary ingredients and their ratio that make gunpowder – sulphur (1) charcoal (4) saltpetre (6) – were discovered in thirteenth century Europe by an alchemist monk, Roger Bacon. In the mix of a modern match the ingredients of gunpowder do not exist, but with charcoal added to the mix it becomes a reasonable explosive. And by the end of the next week we had a confined space ready for it.

Masonry bits are regularly used by maintenance crews in prison to bore holes in mortar, and even bluestone, so that metal keepers can be driven in when installing water pipes, electrical conduit, and such. I soon recruited a worker in the metal-shop to steal a new masonry bit, but cautioned him to be subtle; a search for it might upset our plans. While he worked on an excuse to gain access to the locked and guarded tool cabinet, I approached the best artist in B-division and told him what the guy in the metal-shop wanted made out of a piece of dowel I handed him, along with two one-ounce packets of tobacco (the prison currency). The very next morning I had a perfect replicated masonry bit, carved and painted so realistically that cement powder seemed to be visible on the cutting-piece and shaft; a perfect substitute for the real one soon to be taken.

When lined up for a breakfast ladle of porridge and a piece of toast, a daily one-ounce ration of sugar (28 grams) was issued at the same time in a twist of paper, like a skinny ice-cream cone, and a ration of powdered milk came in a similar cone, only half the size. These paper cones were an essential part of the tea drinking ritual which occurred daily throughout the prison (tea leaves filched from the kitchen and even contraband coffee were carried to and fro in them by inmates) and constantly caused disruptions during searches. To open a cone, or not to open it, was always a touchy issue for a screw because of the food factor; and the bitter arguments and threats generated generally dissuaded screws over time from opening them. This was the way I took the fake bit down . . . and also the following day how I brought the real bit back up. To have been caught would have meant at least a week of hard labour, breaking rocks in the punishment division, and no remissions for that month.

Of course the luxury of an electric drill was out of the question, but a hand-driven one was easily constructed. Unlike the metal kind with gear cogs and a handle to generate speed and ease, this one consisted of a curved piece of plywood, a shoelace and a small block of hardwood. It *was* primitive, but it did the job. Copied from a device predating matches and even flint, an animal sinew strung to a bent branch of wood rapidly spun a hardwood stick back and forth on a piece of dry softwood, pressed firmly in place with a flat river stone: back and forth it spun in the softwood until it grew so hot that it spontaneously ignited. By operating the device slightly differently, forward with downward pressure applied to the bit by the wooden block, but eased off when spun back (it would blunt the bit if the pressure stayed on). Forward under pressure as the bit spun . . . and then back with no pressure. . .

Because I made it, you can guess I was the bunny who had to

go in behind the blanket and be first to test it out. The moment I squeezed in behind the dusty blanket, I felt claustrophobic and vulnerable: the very reason I had shouldered other roles to avoid working on the wall. With the radio blaring music and a few crims placed strategically about the shop ready to intercept a roving screw and talk crap if necessary, there was no real risk of being heard or detected; but nevertheless the whirr of the lace, and the grinding bit set my teeth on edge each time I stroked it. And my paranoia kicked in big time lying with my ear next to the cold floor where every approaching footstep was magnified tenfold, into the tread, tread, tread of screws coming to get me.

In just under the hour time-limit for each crim working behind the blanket, I had bored to a depth of one centimetre (an electric drill would have done that in ten seconds) and whispered quiet praise of my invention when I came out for a cup of tea and a sit down. My left shoulder ached from working the bow, and neck muscles I never knew I had constantly felt ready to cramp.

After walking the shop floor to reassure any screw who might subconsciously have missed me, I sat with the card players and unrolled the 'cigarette' of match-head mix (now dry and hard) to crush back into a powder again. Four-fifths of the mix went into a new shape slightly thicker and shorter than a cigarette, to better match the hole, while the remaining fifth became a thin fuse of twisted cigarette papers a few centimetres long. Both were concealed between wooden beams in the loom and remained there undisturbed until needed.

Another centimetre of depth was gained that day and three more the next, a total of five centimetres, but still I knew it was not enough. The friction the bluestone on the shank of the bit, and the work the tip had already done, affected its ability to cut; it was virtually blunt. But by frequent hammering of a thin bolt in the hole to roughen the bottom, the bit continued to cut, though grudgingly. Another two centimetres were gained until it became obvious another drill would be needed if we were to continue drilling.

Rather than make the call myself, I put it to a vote (crims are quick to shift the blame when a thing fails): charge the hole at seven centimetres, or delay till the following week and procure another drill. As anticipated, everyone involved wanted it to go ahead – the mental pressure had become too much for some and it was beginning to show. In particular Big John, who was vital to the escape, an armed robber of banks and armoured vans whose crimes were quick and over and done with in just a few action-filled minutes, was increasingly unable to cope with the drawn-out nature of this escape. On the other hand a few in the coir-shop were not visibly stressed, mentally adapted to this kind of protracted risk. The duration and the few bursts of stress had no cumulative effect on them at all.

Four months earlier a screw had accepted payment of a small fortune to smuggle in a revolver. Unknown to him an escape was planned to go out through the administration section with hostages taken. That plot never reached fruition: it was trampled when a trusted prisoner working there jumped the queue and walked out through the front gate bold as brass disguised as a Visitor (good people who give their time to prisoners from interstate or have no family to visit them). The gun remained in BJ's possession, but without a purpose and every day at risk of being found in a security ramp: until he learnt of our plan.

John knew the first few up the ladder had to be very agile to have any chance of getting the drop on the screw before he could un-sling his rifle, and being a large man his only condition when offering the gun was that he be in the first four. With a handgun available to storm the tower (and not a short stabbing spear as originally planned) it would be a cert, so of course he got fourth place. Originally I had claimed fourth, but was happy to step back and take fifth spot instead. So, the first four up the ladder would be determined armed robbers familiar with speed and threat. The *forte* of a safe-breaker such as me is endurance and stealth, but those qualities had no part to play in the taking of an armed tower guard. I listened and learned.

The block of bluestone in the yard could not be worked on; any activity out of the ordinary would quickly alert an observant prison guard wandering the division. As a result of that restraint everything hinged on our ability to remove the bluestone block in the coir-shop to gain access to the yard-block from *within* the wall. The mortar in two sides and the top holding the yard-block in place could be removed (the bottom course had been removed decades ago) with no chance of discovery from the yard side, leaving the last visible centimetre or so in the external wall until break-out day. Our escape plan steam-rolled ahead.

The cracking of the rock had everyone worried. All kinds of concerns were voiced. How loud would it be? Would the building shake? Are pieces of rock likely to be blown out like shrapnel from an exploding grenade into the crowded coir-shop? All were unknowns. I theorised and said from my experience when blowing a safe, a small charge of gelignite the same size as the one we were contemplating sounded like a cracker going off; not excessively loud at all. (If that small charge failed to blow the lock-box, then a charge ten times that size went in to remove the door.)

A contest of strength was organised for the next day, to determine who was the strongest in the shop, lifting one side of the smallest loom and not dropping it until after a count of three. Of course doing that would cause a loud noise and vibrate the floor – which just happened to be what was needed to disguise the gunpowder charge when it went off. We hoped we were right

. . . with fingers crossed.

Behind the curtain I toiled in the cramped space, carefully tamping the charge to the bottom of the hole with the fuse attached; no one else in the shop knew how to. (In the land of the blind, a one-eyed man is king.) And when satisfied, I screwed a small brass tap with the fuse woven out through the spout into the hole, making it airtight. Gunpowder will burn rapidly if exposed to air – not explode – and all would have been a wasted effort. When I appeared amidst the card players again everyone knew what to expect. The atmosphere felt electric.

Pete was to be the fuse lighter, a madcap desperado who once shot a pizza man in the foot for not putting enough anchovies on his order. He delighted in the opportunity to blow something up, who viewed the dangerous task as exciting. Pete was champing at the bit and held ready a broom handle with a burning cigarette lighter tied to the end waiting for my go-ahead. The card game which never stopped, even when a fight occurred, was hastily abandoned; all the players at the same time said they needed to go take a piss. I backed up a few paces too, out of the line of fire to where I could watch Pete and give the weightlifting team the nod to start their fake contest.

The loom rose . . . and I dropped my hand like a race starter's flag to Pete. Like a conjuror he thrust the burning stick behind the blanket and concentrated on the task of lighting the fuse. Two seconds passed . . . THUMP went the loom and the floor of the building vibrated under my feet! But mentally, I registered no explosion. A fucking dud, I screamed to myself. And looked at Pete to get an idea of what had gone wrong. The look of disappointment on his dial would have been comical if not for the seriousness of the matter.

The overseer stepped out of his office and hurried with the two shop screws towards the loom-lifting team to have words with them. Feeling dejected, I sat and waited for the card players to return and fill the loom before ducking behind the blanket to assess what had gone wrong, forgetting in the moment of woe how dangerous that could have been if the fuse was a hang-fire and still smouldering.

The tap was missing so I knew immediately that force from the gunpowder had ejected it, but the rest had yet to be discovered. Hunched over disappointedly, I stared at the hole that had taken us days to drill in the stone block until my eyes fully adjusted to the darkness – hairline fractures radiated from the hole. The deflagration had cracked it! Two lines out to one side and a third went straight down. The match-heads had performed better than a quarryman wielding a sledge hammer could ever have done! I popped my head out and chortled an enthusiastic, "It did it!" Before pulling back to investigate more.

A buzz of excited whisperings spread like a wave throughout the shop. We were back in business. Each piece of the broken rock moved when pushed, not a lot, but enough to allow judicious levering to remove one of the top pieces. After that the other two parts of the stone were a piece of cake to drag out. Apart from a few large segments of bluestone rubble in the wall cavity, the yard-block was clearly revealed. And we now had a far safer place to store our tools. When I got a tap on the shoulder indicating that my hour was up and time to swap, it seemed as though only ten minutes had passed, so elated I felt. Pacing the workshop floor I disciplined myself to maintain normality despite the thrilling experience.

Two days later, walking through the division, I heard a commotion in two-yard and immediately changed direction to investigate; it might have had something to do with our venture. I stood in the gateway and scanned the yard expecting to learn what the disturbance was before entering. A young guy rushed towards me, followed by two others in hot pursuit. I stepped aside to avoid contact and he ran down five-tier to disappear into a cell. The ones chasing him were Keith and Cos, a dodgy duo he should not have crossed.

In the yard I walked directly to where four men congregated in the far corner. Another squatted at their feet with his back pressed against our bluestone block! It wasn't half obvious that they were trying to conceal the block of bluestone.

"What do you guys thinks you're doing?", I immediately inquired, kicking the one on the concrete in the leg, telling him to get him up.

He stayed seated. One of the standing men answered for him, a man vouched for as staunch, and therefore I listened to him before taking it further. This was serious stuff: out of the hundred and twenty inmates in B, only a handful knew of this hiding spot and how important it had become as a focal point to quite a few.

"We were told to watch it; something came up." Only shivs for the escape were kept there, and Keith and Cos must have been getting one out when the young guy twigged to it. So they chased him. I read the situation as dicey, and thought it best not to wait.

"I'm closing it!" No ifs or buts as I squatted down to put in place a thin wooden strip made to look and fit exactly in place of the missing mortar. It only took a moment and it was done. "Tell no one of this stash," I warned them, again saying it for emphasis, "No one!" I walked away, angry over the carelessness of what had just happened.

An hour later, the sound of loud voices in the division drew me out of the small hobby shop (a converted office) to learn that a security screw was in the division ordering a struggling prisoner being held by two wing officers, to stand still. The prisoner was Keith. As I went to leave the area for a less conspicuous spot to watch from and learn what was going down, the chief of security rushed through the main gateway, held open for him by one of the wing officers, into the spacious circle with a squad of six black-clad henchmen behind him.

As he approached Keith, he gave orders to the squad following, "Make every prisoner stay exactly where they are, and not to move." The four or five inmates within hearing of that order were galvanised to flee, me included.

"Stop those prisoners!" he yelled at the top of his voice to the men in black fanning out around him. One quickly grabbed me by the arm and another fleeing prisoner nearby was also grabbed by his arm, but being older and in for murder serving life, Jack was very sure of himself, and said menacingly to the screw that held him, "Get ya fucking hand off me or I'll punch ya in the face!" The screw let go as though bitten by a ferret. Jack stormed away towards his cell on tier six.

As I pulled unsuccessfully to free my arm, a shocked cry of pain came from where the screws were restraining Keith and so I instantly looked his way to see if it was him who had been hurt. If I had delayed looking by a nanosecond I would have missed seeing the fist of Keith withdraw after having struck the security chief's nose full on. The Chief staggered back a step, then another step as a moan of pain escaped his lips, clutching his face while blood dripped all down the front of his perfectly pressed uniform. His hat lay at his feet trampled out of shape, covered in his own blood. The screw holding me let go and lifted his arms in a defensive boxing pose, shocked by the violence, and then leapt to the aid of his compatriots to help subdue Keith. Something *really* serious must have happened to warrant this wild response. I was out of there.

Security took over divisional control, with additional screws streaming in from nearby divisions summonsed to help quell the tumultuous situation. An almost riotous period with fifty or so angry and vocal men in each yard locked down and isolated, not being told why, until sufficient manpower arrived to calm the division down. Each prisoner was formally identified and their name recorded as they entered the division before being escorted to their cell and locked away, conclusively establishing by elimination the names of the fifteen or twenty prisoners in the division at the time of the attack. When concluded the gates into both exercise yards were again locked, allaying some of my misgivings. If two-yard had been the only gate locked it would have indicated that they knew something of our plot, meaning an informer existed.

Before long the true cause of the disturbance (not the broken nose incident blown out of proportion as I thought it to be) had travelled like smoke throughout the division. A prisoner on five-tier had been murdered, stabbed repeatedly and left on the slate floor of his cell to die slowly in an expanding pool of his own blood. His body lay there, locked in a cell by the wing screw that discovered him, waiting for the homicide squad and forensic team to arrive. And that explained why such an unusual rigmarole had been needed when putting the division into a lockdown: a murder protocol had been conducted.

Under interrogation, by making everyone account for who they saw and where they were, a process of elimination using corroborative evidence winnows out the innocent in a pool of suspects, leaving the guilty in the remaining few. That eliminative technique works well in society where people obey the law and want to assist the police, but those tactics did not work that way on this day.

A core of belligerent inmates refused to cooperate, keeping the pool of suspects large, thereby making it difficult for the police to discover the guilty. But by taking that course it made me an equal suspect, along with twenty or so others until we were eliminated during the investigation (no explanation given). Our escape plan was shelved for a while, constantly teetering on a knife edge of detection, until the disruption caused by the murder investigation eventually wound down a fortnight later when two inmates were officially charged with murder. The prison routines returned to normal once again.

Throughout the time taken implementing the escape, the most difficult obstacle to overcome barring our way had been two short lengths of stout chain used to secure the side gate that faced the tower. A large obsolete padlock from an earlier prison era with the hasp opening on a hinge (not in and out like a modern lock does) connected the chains – suggesting that once long ago it had failed to open, requiring a link to be cut, but parsimoniously retained as a permanent join of the chain to allow its continued use.

The two pieces of chain and connecting padlock were barely long enough to reach around the first bar of the gate, through a steel grill on the wall and then back to be joined on itself with a modern top-shelf quality padlock. The overseer inspected this locked gate at least once during every working day, and his random action prevented us from cutting a link or a bar in that circumstance, even though two hi-speed hacksaw blades hidden in the shop were originally smuggled in for that purpose. For everyone involved, the mass escape hinged on the gate impasse being solved. The finished ladder waited *in situ*, the pieces ready to be gathered and assembled on the day. Like me, a few inmates had procured colourful civilian shirts and stashed them in readiness to wear when going over the wall.

The gate problem frustrated my sanity, unable to move on, until out of the blue a solution in the form of a boastful burglar arrived in B-division. Wannabes and boasters were always challenged (to put them in their place) and so this guy was made to prove his boast that he could open any lock, or from then on to keep his loud mouth shut. When taken to the hobby room and shown a small padlock on a tool cabinet and told that he had an hour to do it (everyone who frequented that room had a go at picking it) he surprised everyone by using a piece of curved tinfoil cut from a discarded drink can, slipping it down the hasp to push back the ball bearing and actually opened it in less than a minute! (Springing a lock, even a simple one, is not as easy as commonly believed.) Given suitable reasons why, and with a few helpful hints of what might happen if he refused, he requested assignment to the coir shop. And the new friends he now had convinced the divisional chief that the coir shop was the best place for him.

Within three days of his arrival apprised of our lock problem (but no mention of the escape plot that hinged on the outcome), stationed at the gate with a lever and pick of his own manufacture, and half a dozen determined crims watching his back ready to protect him from detection, he set to it like his quality of life depended on a quick outcome, (and in some ways it did). The top-grade padlock resisted his every attempt to open it (unlike the simple one in the division) no matter how hard he tried. By the start of his second week, using a 'donated' tattoo gun he had converted into a crude flicker (a vibration device used by burglars to jump the pins in a cylinder), he still could not open it.

Acknowledging defeat, he tried the ancient padlock; for hours he fiddled away unsuccessfully at the levers inside (as we all had in idle moments) until finally he went in search of a long piece of wire to use as a probe when he said he was encountering resistance on the third lever where resistance should not be. It was Greek to me but I told him to solve it as a lot of people were depending on him and failure was not acceptable. He understood the unspoken message.

The next day he showed me a small clump of packing lead in the palm of his hand – like black vermicelli – which explained the cause of why the lock could not be opened way back, when the decision was made by a turnkey (as screws were called in the nineteenth century) to cut the chain. A troubled convict had vandalised the lock, probably to get back at the prison system, preventing free movement of the levers with a key inside. (I suspect the convict never dreamed that his rebellious act would one day pay a dividend!)

"So, can you open it or not?" I eventually asked. That was the only thought filling my mind: the bottom line.

"For sure!" he boasted. "But I've never opened one so old."

I snapped, "Well, how do you know you can do it?" Adding nastily, "You couldn't open the other one when you said you could." His cockiness frustrated me.

"I'm good at this shit," he again boasted, glossing over his earlier failure, "so something old like that won't beat me." He tipped his hand to let the strands of lead fall to the floor, the cause of our impasse found, leaving me to catch up mentally while he headed back to the gate and the group of men pretending to have an interest in a card game set up in the gateway to catch the cool breeze. (That was the excuse given when the vigilant overseer noticed the change in habit and asked why they were all sitting there.)

Just like he said, the old lever padlock on the chain turned out to be easy! Now that all the lead had been removed his efforts at unlocking it was quickly rewarded; at the end of the working day, to demonstrate his lock-picking proficiency, he twice opened and closed it in quick succession! The escape was now a reality; all we had to do was decide on a date. My heart started to palpitate just visualising it, so who knew what it would do to me on the day pumped full of adrenalin.

The hostage part of the plan was already solved and in place. A small group of well-intentioned Visitors entered the prison every weekend, invited into each division to sit with troubled inmates and discuss ways to deal with probable social encounters when released. A slim middle-aged woman was often in the group, and we figured a tower guard would be swayed by a female hostage more so than if it were a male, so that was the tack we took.

The strategy to make this plan workable *must* lure the guard out of his tower along the walkway to yard-two, away from the telephone and siren button. A fight in the yard between inmates at first seemed to be the preferred way, but fights were not uncommon and might not keep him entertained long enough, distracted convincingly to allow time for the real prong of the attack to work. But a female Visitor struggling in the grasp of a sex-crazed prisoner with excitable crims verbally provoking the incident would definitely keep his attention focused for the few vital minutes needed while a dozen armed criminals (the first one brandishing a revolver to control him from a distance) climbed a ladder to gain the catwalk at the unseen end. And that woman was already in B-division, willing, and able to assist in every way.

One of the would-be escapees was a bold catamite who favoured a screw to smuggle in eyeliner and lipstick, rather than contraband with trade value, and often dressed as a stripper to entertain crypto gays. He agreed that being held hostage in drag was the way for him to go. And the female disguise when 'her' turn came to go over the wall – skirt, blouse, and face make-up – would probably be the best defence of all against being pin-pointed by a rifle sight. The other nearby tower guards, once alerted to the attack, would be ignorant of the true circumstances of what was unfolding and most unlikely to take a shot at a woman: she might be a hostage forced to climb the ladder cruelly used as a shield for the men behind her.

+ + + +

A mate came to me with a problem, concerned that a kitchen worker two cells up from him was voicing threats and speculating. Based on the words overheard, talk that touched on our endeavour, I went straight to his cell to find out what he knew or suspected. Five minutes later, I abruptly left him in the middle of a rant about 'No one will get me, and if you're one of them, I'll stab ya!' I wanted to leave him with the impression that his threat had scared me.

He knew nothing about our escape plan, fortunately, but was so paranoid over inmates whispering when he came near and activity he had observed in the division that he took our preparations for the escape, the making and passing of shivs and other oddments, as centred on him. Guilt will wreak strange thoughts in an unnatural environment and is so compelling sometimes that murder has been committed based on a misunderstood look. He had to go before he jeopardised our plan by attacking one of us, and I intended to play on his own negative paranoia to accomplish it.

Persuasive methods employed in prison are basic and therefore limited to hostility, threats, violence, and harsher outcomes, used equally by both the screws and by the inmates. Fear and pain is the form regularly resorted to and what most expect. I intended to go outside the norm and use a variation – subterfuge. A harmless act dressed in violence to appear far worse than it actually seemed. A sheep in wolf's clothing, to turn the phrase around. I was sure his disturbed mind would fill in the blanks, and do the rest for me.

The makings of what I wanted, was already in the division and close to hand; all I had to do was gather the pieces and assemble it. A scare was all he needed, not a physical assault that would needlessly put me or someone else at risk. Plus, it would misdirect and give the screws something else to think about. If this gambit failed, and only then, would I notch it up a rung. First, I had to make a bomb.

It might sound easy to someone not screwed under a constant heel of intimidation but in prison, where *everything* is suspect and broken rules attract punishments, one needs to weigh every action carefully if they hope to survive their sentence unscathed. I did that, as I sourced a length of string, a jar, a rubber band and a thumbtack, three matches, and a striker strip torn from a new matchbox. The glass jar was placed in my locker with a small amount of jam inside (empty jars were an offence to keep) so that if ramped that night the jar would be overlooked in the search as separate from the other odd pieces scattered around my cell.

Before the morning bell to rise had rung, I rinsed the jar clean and half filled it with sweepings from the floor (to simulate an explosive mixture). With the striker strip bent in two and the matches held securely between the bent strips by the rubber band, I attached one end of the string to the matches before running it and the very ends of the matches through a hole punched in the lid. The strip of striker stayed in the jar, too large to fit through the hole. When pulled by the string those matches would scrape the striker and flare into a burst of flame, but failing to ignite the 'explosive' mixture, sufficient to put the wind up anyone who triggered the action by opening the drawer where I intended to affix it.

The moment my cell door opened at let-out I walked direct to where this crim lived knowing, like everyone else, that he should be lined up for breakfast. After confirming that he stood in line and a nod from my mate behind him, I stepped into his cell and thumb-tacked the loose end of the short string to the underside of his locker's top with the drawer barely open. It was crudely assembled and unlikely to have worked even if the 'explosive' material was real, but this was a mind-game intended to spark fear in the victim, not rational thought. I left his cell the moment it was done and stood in the breakfast queue to collect two pieces of cold toast.

Breakfast finished and time moved on, but no response was visible from where I sat in my mate's cell watching. When the bell rang for the work gangs to assemble in yard-one, his door remained closed and I had to leave before learning an outcome. In the industrial area I wondered until lunchtime when, on entering the division again, I knew something had finally happened. The division was akin to an anthill disturbed and rife with rumour over why a screw stood guard outside a locked cell. After a few inquiries, I learnt that the crim from that cell had left the building under escort, shouting threats at everyone he saw.

Because the loud-mouth worked in the kitchen, his hours were different, so after assisting the delivery of lunch to B-division he could relax there until again required to pick up and deliver the evening meal. He grabbed his lunch and went to his cell. The rest I learned from Happy, the divisional sweeper, an eyewitness who described the events with a fair amount of vivid drama woven through it all. However, out of his exaggerated version I winkled these facts.

No sooner had the loser entered his cell than he burst back out screaming that a bomb had gone off in his locker. Happy almost dropped his lunch, shocked by the outburst he said, but had heard nothing except this person yelling his lungs off that someone had tried to murder him. (With only floor sweepings in the jar that would have taken some doing, but no doubt the flaring matches as hoped had given him sufficient fright.)

Two circle screws rushed to find out what he was on about, while the third one grabbed the phone and tried to halt the returning work-gangs: but too late, the gangs were already on their way. He joined the other two wing screws after they backed out of the cell, both nodding their heads in unison, with one saying, "There's something in there all right!" They immediately locked the cell door and hastily left the scene. All the prisoners standing around, drawn by the activity and hearing what the screw said edged away from the cell area as well.

The senior screw in charge prudently ordered the wing to be guarded until the bomb squad arrived. Moreover, as each work-gang entered the division and collected their lunch, the inmates on that tier were banned from entering their cells and were told to eat out in the yards. I arrived towards the end: it was quite interesting, listening to the speculations and the grumblings and disputes that went on.

Earlier than the usual hour given for lunch, the bell rang again to muster in yard-one and the work-gangs were quickly sent back to the industrial area. Happy said the cops arrived after that, carrying bags of forensic gear and such. And were in the cell for less than twenty minutes before they left: a screw whispered to Happy that the 'bomb' had been a hoax, and the cops were pissed off because of their wasted time. It pleased me to hear that. Mission accomplished without bloodshed and only a few feathers ruffled.

+ + + +

The day and time to go was set: Saturday, just after 11:00 am, when the morning movie ended in the divisional chapel. The tower guard was at the end of his shift waiting to be relieved, bored and fatigued, when the bustle of preparations for bringing lunch for two hundred men from the communal kitchen got underway. And outside the prison, organised through different crews, willing allies had parked two stolen vans at prearranged spots to ensure that a vehicle would be where we expected it, depending on which way the circumstances forced us to flee. Our wannabe tough lock-picker, scared shitless now that he knew about the escape and by the thought of being trapped in the coir-shop after crawling through the hole in the wall to open the padlock with recklessly armed men possibly blocking his return, pleaded to be allowed to open it Friday afternoon instead before the coir-shop was emptied and securely locked for the coming weekend. He got his way, rather than we risk his nerves failing to open the lock because of fourteen angry men breathing down his neck.

When the call came to leave the coir-shop Friday afternoon, under cover of grabbing coats and personal stuff before lining up to be searched and marched out, the old padlock in the chain was unlocked, then held closed and efficiently tied with very fine copper-wire to maintain the semblance of security when peered at or even shaken. We filed out in pairs for the count, with me last to confirm whether the gate was locked behind me. Additional searches were sometimes requested by the overseer, conducted when vacant, and the front gate left unlocked was the giveaway. The two shop screws escorted us the short distance to the B-division entrance, while the overseer disappeared back inside!

The moment we were released to the division I worriedly explained to a few of the others what had happened. All were on tenterhooks after that, discussing every angle we could think of, making it worse by the theories and fears that were thrown about, until the lock-up bell rang. All that night in bed I tossed and turned, not only wondering why the overseer re-entered the coir-shop, but rehashing over and over what could go wrong during the escape. Long-timers had told me of daylight escape attempts to scale the walls of Pentridge: none had ever succeeded as a group. A few had been shot at and even wounded for getting too close to the wall after breaching the security fence into dead-man's land – the four-metre strip of earth between the barbed-wire fence and the actual bluestone wall the towers perched upon like beasts of prey waiting for game to venture near – and a nineteen year old was shot through both lungs (dead before he hit the ground) when he tried with a grappling hook to climb a rarely-used gate opposite A-division, the longest section of wall between towers in the entire Pentridge perimeter. And that was a comparatively easy spot to assault compared to the security measures in place with four towers surrounding maximum security B-division. My mind was in a whirl when in the wee hours of Saturday morning I finally collapsed into restorative sleep.

The altered routine of would-be escapees throughout the division was evident and disruptive, alerting all who were not in the know to the fact that something heavy was going down; with me unintentionally adding to the drama after breakfast by hastening from member to member cautioning them to act normal by going to the movie, or their changed behaviour would be latched onto by the perambulating screws as suspicious. My advice went unheeded; the tension for some was so overwhelming that they avoided the breakfast line-up and resorted to walking up and down in yard-two at a rapid pace to release pent-up energy. It was impossible for me and a few like-minded others to stem the anomaly. Like a beast made up of many parts, it had acquired a life of its own. When the projectionist arrived with his escort screw and three canisters of film I exercised remarkable restraint by following them upstairs to the chapel door where about twenty others congregated like docile sheep, and waited until a wing screw climbed the stairs to unlock it.

As usual, moviegoers escorted from E and C divisions filed into the chapel in two groups. Being locked in a dark room with about eighty other moviegoers spread through the pews, seated on an uncomfortable wooden bench for two hours enduring a tedious movie, seemed endless. Not knowing what was happening in the division took remarkable willpower and fortitude, believe me! Before the lights came on at the end of the show our group rose as one and sped past the projector still running through the credits, headed for the door, where we were forced to wait because of our haste, with our minds churning, while the wing screw took his time getting up to open it.

Even with my eyes squinted to adjust to the brightness of the circle – mid-morning sunlight beamed in through the glass panes of the cupola above – I knew shit had hit the fan when I saw black-clad security screws roaming about below! And the most distressing sight (and for me the bleakest) was yard-two's gate padlocked shut, with a security screw standing guard. The yard visible through the bars, normally filled with inmates and lots of activity, appeared starkly empty. A feeling of devastation washed over me: after all the effort I had put in and the travails dealt with, the game was over.

Without wasting time on regret, I yelled the name of a prisoner in the grip of a security screw (my subconscious working overtime to protect my arse). "Pete, what the fuck is going on, mate?" The moviegoers hanging over the rail were equally surprised and intently interested in the answer, too.

Being a man who could think on his feet, Pete responded before the screw holding him had time for any input. "I think there was going to be a skirmish with a few from E if they came over for the movie." (E-division was used to divide gang members and co-accused and that manipulative practice constantly caused friction.) And of course Pete's incisive answer cautioned me that the escape plot had not been uncovered! My hopes again soared.

Down the stairs I raced, along with everyone else from the movie, to be stopped by a cluster of security screws at the bottom intent on taking down our names and discovering where we had suddenly come from. For once I cooperated as a model prisoner;

being in a locked room with two screws and a civilian projectionist to corroborate my alibi made it watertight for me if anything bad emerged out of this. The moment I got free of the stairwell I raced to the radio room on six-tier (where the B-division music came from) to find out from Peter, the radio man, what had happened to bring security into it so quickly.

The divisional chief had been alerted by his men that something was astir: the small number of moviegoers from B-division, and the unusual activity and the concentration of men in yard-two confirmed that something drastic was about to erupt. He ordered yard-two's gate locked with the men still in it, and called the tower guard to cover them with his rifle until security arrived. What I stepped into was the aftermath of yard-two being emptied and a few prisoners held for questioning over a number of weapons found discarded in the yard. (The film's soundtrack had blocked out all of the angry voices and noise made during the mini-lockdown.)

Incredibly the revolver that this plot pivoted on remained hidden during two back-to-back yard searches: wrapped in plastic, it hung by a length of twine inside a sewer pipe. (Smuggled back out of the prison soon after this event, that revolver was used eighteen months later in Adelaide to shoot a man in the head, unbelievable as it may seem, though not connected to this story. The shooter (Les), who was in B at the time of this escape attempt, got a life sentence for that crime.)

The second search was far more thorough and successful than the first, very disappointing for all involved in the escape plot. It was the undoing of everything. When located, the removable block of bluestone kept the yard locked for a week while hectic repairs were carried out in both the yard and the coir-shop. The breadth of the plot foiled by chance only hours away from execution staggered the prison authorities. Yet the media never got a whiff of it. Every name on the list of who was in yard-two when locked down underwent rough questioning by security, and a few ended up in the punishment division charged with offences, though if my memory serves me right none related to the escape attempt. I was not even a suspect; being a moviegoer had allayed suspicion, and saved me from detection!

+ + + +

15
SNIFFER DOGS

Yatala Prison with garden tower in foreground, B-division in background

ONLY THOSE WHO DARE TO FAIL GREATLY CAN EVER ACHIEVE GREATLY

- Robert F Kennedy

"I can do it, Joe," he said, "if you help me with the gun-tower guard."

"What do you mean?" I asked, unable to grasp his request.

"I can't see which way he's looking when I'm at the wire fence. I need a signal when he's watching outside."

"What? You really think it can be done in a few minutes?"

"For two days, and again this morning," he told me, "the tower guard watched the garden gang for eight minutes without turning." Fritz had an associate in his division who watched for him but could not learn, until his return in the afternoon, what the screw did each morning.

"How do you even know the same screw will be rostered for that tower tomorrow?"

"I don't, Joe. But I think that tower has been ordered to watch until they're locked into the garden compound." That made real sense: two trusty gardeners had made a run for freedom a week earlier, and one of them had actually been able to scale the high boundary fence topped with barbed wire and disappear into the suburb of Northfield dripping a trail of blood, upsetting all the neighbours. Knowing the tower guard's watchful gaze was on them, and mindful of the M1 carbine he carried, it would be a good visual deterrent as a warning to others not to run.

This was the third escape plan that Fritz had put to me in three months. The other two were just too complicated and therefore likely to fail. However, this one's simplicity had merit, relying only on speed and audacity, Fritz having an abundance of both. My place of confinement meant I was unable to join him, not that I wanted to. At close range, a 30-calibre bullet would rip through both lungs, lethal at fifty metres and almost impossible for a shooter to miss and that was how close to the tower Fritz proposed going over the wall!

In B-division, the maximum security wing in Yatala where I lived, all inmate movements in and out of the division were strictly controlled. A-division where Fritz lived had a lower security rating, not withstanding that, it still came under the entire security umbrella of Yatala, allowing him more freedom of movement, one of the reasons we could periodically get together and talk.

The visit by him with me this particular day had been approved by one of the prison chiefs to discuss a court case Fritz had pending. His lawyer had been instructed to subpoena me to his committal hearing, that entitled him to speak with any witness (including me) and he took full advantage of that rule. (There are many ways to flout prison regulations if the threat of discovery or punishment fails to deter.)

I spent my daily activities locked in a yard with twenty or so prisoners serving long terms, constantly watched by an armed guard in a gun-tower. On the other hand, Fritz worked in the prison kitchen preparing vegetarian meals (originally employed as a scullery hand, he had convinced the overseer that he was qualified to do the job). That meant an early morning start with a few other kitchen staff, but because of his separate and unusual duties, he worked alone and the screws in the kitchen lost track of where he was. After all, where could an inmate go once locked in the kitchen? His plan relied on that lax belief.

The action Fritz required of me needed sorting out and agreed to in this hour contact: he could not wangle another legal visit for at least a fortnight. The crucial task for me therefore, was how to let him know when the guard in the tower had his back towards the inner prison.

Quick thought, as well as direct action, is a prerequisite of survival if incarcerated. If you ponder over a response too much, your opponent will interpret hesitation as weakness and get the first punch in. For that reason, I voiced the first idea that came to mind. "A signal from the top tier, higher than the tower, would do it. How many windows can you see facing the tower on the way to the kitchen?"

Fritz closed his eyes and said, "Five on the top, and three on the second floor." He had a wizard recall. The clothing store roof obscured the ground floor windows, and the entry wing of B-division blocked most of the windows of the upper floors. Prison buildings are intentionally built close by design, yet separate.

"John is somewhere near the end. He'll do it."

"What will it be?"

"A shirt hung out the moment the screw turns his back. And if he looks around the shirt comes back in. What do you think?"

He gave it considerable thought. 'Yeah, that will do," Fritz finally said, "but I need to know that the scaffolding is finished."

"Okay; the shirt only comes out if the screw's back is turned *and* the scaffolding looks complete."

"Yeah; that's good."

His plan relied on two unusual circumstances occurring together. Maintenance on the prison wall for the first time in years was happening that week. And the nearest tower guard watched the garden escort each morning to the exclusivity of everything else.

Looking from outside the prison, the height of the perimeter wall from top to ground level varied from five metres to six depending on the terrain. Connecting fences and a variety of obstacles meant a vehicle could not circle in close to the prison. Inside the prison, though, the ground was levelled like a football field before construction of the cellblocks had begun and therefore the wall height was the same five-metre level consistently all the way round.

Five metres in from the wall a high cyclone-wire fence existed with coiled barbed wire along the top to prevent anyone from approaching the wall. An unauthorised person sighted in that 'no go' zone would be immediately challenged by one of the tower guards and ran the very real risk of being shot. Patrolling prison guards in blue uniforms could circle inside the prison between the wall and fence unobstructed except for where the imposing front entrance building into Yatala intruded. This now brings me to explain the reference and worry Fritz made concerning scaffolding.

Because of escapees in the past using ropes and hooks as a means to scale the wall an ingenious yet simple security measure had been added to the wall. Something I have not seen or heard of in any other prison. Three endless rows of unmortared building bricks were stacked on a mortared bottom row atop the wall. A grappling hook thrown anywhere along the length of the wall to snag the top would bring down a cascade of bricks! Along with the noise the gap at the top and the bricks below would indicate to the alerted guards exactly where the escape had been attempted. A half-dozen spots visible on the wall where bricks were missing each had a story to tell.

In addition, the old barbed wire barriers protecting the prison towers needed renewal. External contractors with scaffolding progressively moved from site to site inside the wall and cyclone-wire fence, and were attending to the job of replacing the barb with a deadly innovation aptly named razor-wire that would slice and dice the hands and arms of any prisoner foolish enough to handle it without proper protection. The scaffolding had been dismantled that day. It had stood under the tower for three days fitting the razor-wire, and was being re-erected fifty metres past the tower to replace a section of missing bricks on top of the wall, and presumably it would be fully assembled ready to continue work the next day.

The breach atop the wall to be restacked with bricks was almost a metre wide. An area was exposed five years earlier by a determined escapee who thought he could carefully hook all the bricks down to eventually snag his hook on one of the mortared bricks at the bottom of the pile, scale the wall, and flee the prison before a patrolling guard arrived. In theory a good idea, but unfortunately he miscalculated the volume of noise the falling bricks generated at three o'clock in the morning, and what two determined guards with 455 Webley revolvers would do to ensure that they remained employed.

Fritz intended to take advantage of that gap. Not easy, but he had the guts and the ability to pull it off provided he kept his nerve and stayed focused. Any intruding thought of being shot dead by the tower guard would erode his resolve.

"I'm worried I will lose my nerves, Joe," uttered Fritz, voicing my very thoughts!

"Concentrate on the shirt," I advised him. "John won't let you down. Don't even think of looking at the tower." An easy thing for me to say, I know. It always is easy to talk tough when not taking the risk yourself.

"What time do you leave A-division?" I asked.

"At six thirty every morning. The overseer and a kitchen screw escort us. The rest arrive after eight."

"And then what?"

"I won't enter the kitchen; they don't count us going in." Another mental blind spot because they had already counted them coming out of A-division only minutes before. Fritz would take advantage of their oversight.

"So you'll have to stay hidden longer than an hour?" The more I heard, the more worried I felt for Fritz. The garden trusties were escorted outside the prison and handed over to their overseers ten minutes earlier than the divisional musters, so that the screws could return in time to assist with the hectic eight o'clock escort movements within the prison. Not until after the work gangs were locked in their places of labour were the contractors working on the wall allowed to enter the prison to continue their job. Quite a handful to juggle, and if Fritz got it wrong they would hunt him down and lock him in the dreaded S-division for a term of punishment. (In those days, it was both mental *and* physical.)

"Have you got a spot to hide picked out where the top tier can be seen?" If not, I figured his whole plan failed.

"I will find somewhere. I have an hour to do it." His confidence came from an inborn arrogance, yet without that arrogance, he would not be able to pull it off. At least in the morning at that time, between six thirty and eight, only a few screws moved about the prison, going to their rostered workplaces for the day. Even if he daringly stood in the open, provided he acted normal and was doing something, it was likely he would go unchallenged.

The screw who escorted Fritz to B-division walked towards us. He said, "Five minutes, so finish up." He walked back to stand by the gate to wait for Fritz.

The wing screw strolled up to unlock the gate and let them out. Before the gate had been relocked, I had already rushed off in search of John and found him just as the bell for dinner rang out. In the mess-room, my gums were going non-stop and I don't mean eating. John was a little overwhelmed to have such responsibility thrown at him, but he stepped up. Fritz could not have asked for a more staunch and reliable ally. The dice would roll: win . . . lose . . . draw. One out of three ain't bad.

That night was a restless one for me, knowing Fritz would give his best effort in the morning, wondering what the wash-up would be. A few times during the night, I stood on the locker and stared through the cell bars at the section of brightly-lit wall visible from my cell on the second floor, no scaffolding or tower in sight, trying to imagine what Fritz would face. Gradually the dark cell where I lay lit up with rays of early morning sunlight.

The get-up bell rang loud at seven and as always, fifteen minutes later the doors were unlocked and the clangourous tread of leather boots on metal rang out as men streamed down the stairs from the upper tiers towards the food line for breakfast. I tried to enter John's section but the security gates of his wing dividing the division into small control areas stayed locked. That worried me.

By the time his gates were unlocked to allow movement through to the mess, an officious screw had ordered me to grab my breakfast and enter the eating area. John never arrived, and at first, I thought the worst. However, it was not yet eight o'clock. He maintained his vigil until I came looking for him.

Like me the night before, John used his locker to stand on, staring out the barred window, but from where he watched he could see the tower and the guard in it. The moment I stepped into his cell I asked, "Did you see him go?"

John had been so engrossed in what he was doing that he had not heard me enter. Even though I gave him a scare, he never pulled in his shirt, only said, "Fucking knock next time, will you!" and again stared out at the tower.

"I haven't seen anything," he advised. "Are you sure he'll do it?"

"Yeah, he'll do it if it can be done," I confidently stated. "Can you see the whole area?"

"Nope, just A-division where it stops at the cyclone near the tower, and some of the scaffolding." He quickly pulled in his shirt.

"That's it," he said with finality as he stepped off the locker to the floor. "The screw is looking this way now." I sprang onto his locker to gaze out and get an idea of what Fritz faced. The area looked incredibly exposed, and when I saw the fence below, I wondered how Fritz had gotten over the cyclone and barbed-wire.

The divisional bell rang loud; that meant it was time for the eight o'clock muster when every prisoner without exceptions, unless confirmed sick, had to muster in ranks to answer to a roll call. We descended to the ground floor in silence, suspecting that Fritz had failed in his attempt and now lay hidden somewhere inside the prison complex. When time came for the lunchtime meals in the yards and the vegetarians complained that their meals had not arrived, mental alarm bells would ring and a search carried out in the kitchen would reveal that Fritz was missing. And the hunt would be on.

Confined in a crowded security yard as usual – only those who could be trusted not to sabotage got work – my thoughts were with Fritz as the hours crawled by. As predicted, after collecting our lunchtime plates and cutlery a rollcall of the prisoners in each of the security yards took place, instigated by the missing vegetarian meals. It triggered disheartenment and anger in me. I paced the yard, up and down, to relieve my frustration.

By now, a rumour had started, and it is amazing how accurate some jail rumours can nearly be. *An inmate broke out of the kitchen and was hiding in the prison waiting for the cover of night to scale the wall.* Disappointingly, that now seemed to be Fritz's only remaining option. Intending to help him, I added a furphy, hoping to obfuscate the truth of the one currently going round. Inmates are constantly being moved about the prison, in and out of yards, so taking advantage of that activity I knew if enough crims hear from a reliable source (everyone knew Fritz and I were co-accused) it eventually finds its way to the ears of authority.

One of the two escape routes Fritz had mooted I now spread, swearing each prisoner I told to secrecy knowing that as it travelled from ear to ear like Chinese whispers any informer linked in the chain would quickly blab it to security hoping to gain favour. Nothing could be surer.

In no time at all the rumour raced through the prison and came back transformed with minute detail included: *Fritz escaped in the meat truck! After breaking out of the kitchen, he hid between beef carcasses in the meat truck that made a delivery to the prison that very morning. He lifted his feet off the floor and hung from a track when security inspected the truck before allowing it to exit the front gate.* Visibly angered by the event, security carried out another rollcall of the prison, only this time every prisoner was ordered to step forward and be identified; with hecklers in the ranks stirring the pot, it turned into a very frustrating and drawn-out procedure for all involved.

Sniffer dogs were brought in but did not assist with the day-search of the prison: during past escapes, inmates had provoked the animals to upset the handlers whom they abused. To get around that, the prison staff gathered the clothing and bed linen in Fritz's cell and handed it over to the police to conduct an outside search of the fields, and the meat truck, to establish in fact whether he had successfully escaped.

New rumours ran rife, based on information leaked to prisoners. The dogs failed to detect Fritz's scent in the truck when sniffed, and after two circuits of the prison perimeter, the handlers confirmed that their animals had not picked up a scent trail. The police were sure that Fritz was definitely still inside.

That evening back in the division waiting for lock-up, I sat with a few close confederates trying to guess how it might end. We concluded that when the dogs came inside – and they would come in as soon as every prisoner was locked away for the night – it would only be a matter of time before Fritz was winkled out of wherever he was hiding. I consoled my disappointment by recognising that he at least tried, and not just talked about it, as do so many wannabe escapees.

All through the night, I heard the dogs with their trainers urging them on to search the buildings. Even the roofs got a thorough going-over. An incredible amount of effort went into *not* finding him. As morning dawned and the tired dog squads were withdrawn, I concluded that another day of internal searching would commence.

It was funny, really. I found that I suddenly had new friends, prisoners wanting to talk with me, prisoners I barely knew. Security exercising their juvenile cunning had assigned me to a different yard away from established friends hoping that I might be indiscrete and divulge some fact they could use to locate Fritz.

They were as convinced as me that he hid within the prison. Therefore, to retaliate, I firmed up on my original rumour and constantly repeated it: Fritz escaped in the meat truck and was long gone. I never moved from that stance. Security hated me for spreading a slanderous rumour. It reflected very badly on them as they controlled the gate!

The third day of Fritz's uncanny disappearance, prison authorities finally conceded defeat by releasing to the media a short statement acknowledging that a dangerous prisoner had escaped from South Australia's maximum security prison. However, they did add a rider: "Until we know for certain, prison staff will continue to search. He's the kind of bloke who'd lie doggo for days."

It was not until six months later after I escaped from the same prison and joined up with Fritz in a Melbourne caravan park that he explained to me, before heading off together to Queensland, how he actually did it. The authorities never did learn the whole truth. When returned to Yatala six years later to finish the remainder of his interrupted sentence, Fritz refused to divulge any facts on how he had accomplished the impossible. This is how he escaped.

+ + + +

At three in the morning, with a candle-stub burning (no luxury of a light-switch or power-point in prison cells back then) Fritz scrubbed the bluestone walls of his cell with diluted lye stolen from the kitchen. The slate floor came next, and then his wooden locker and door. The stainless steel toilet he concentrated on for ten minutes. Except for two sheets and two blankets folded neatly at the foot of the bed, everything else in the cell – his spare clothing was given to his friend the day before – went into a cardboard box, which he placed next to the door. The neatly folded blankets and sheets he placed on top. The third blanket issued to him on reception had been ripped longways, into two wide strips with one rolled up to take with him and the other he laid under the mattress. Satisfied with what he had done, he relaxed on the bed and waited for the kitchen escort to unlock his door.

"Right-oh, five minutes," the screw said as he swung the door out, and hurried to open another cell further along the dark tier.

Wearing his grey prison jacket to conceal the strip of blanket stuck in his belt, Fritz strolled in his usual manner to the main entrance of A-division where the kitchen overseer waited outside. When the screw returned and unlocked the gate the small group of men stepped out into the dark morning and waited while the screw locked the gate behind them. Every morning as usual, the screw and overseer escorted the group along a winding course to the kitchen. In the rush to enter, no one noticed that Fritz went missing.

The moment he broke from the group when turning a corner, Fritz headed directly to the industrial waste container used by the kitchen. He grabbed one of the cardboard boxes stacked next to it and began collecting the bits of rubbish that had fallen to the ground, pretending it was his clean-up duty for the morning. Quickly working his way around the littered sight, until satisfied that no one observed him, he squeezed in between the container and kitchen wall with the box to conceal him. Until after the divisions roused, he had to remain cramped in that dark space and act like a dormouse. When he heard the wake-up bells ring loud and clear in every division, he knew it was seven o'clock. Forty-five minutes to go.

+ + + +

When the cell doors were unlocked and flung open for the inmates of A-division one prisoner in particular lingered and did not rush out to get his breakfast. Instead, he loitered in his cell until the tier virtually emptied of men before venturing out loaded up with a cardboard box topped with crumpled sheets and blankets.

Carrying the box to a cell not far from his, he entered and closed the door behind him. He quickly covered the bed with his sheets – smelly with body odour, slept in by him for a week – and threw a pair of skid-marked undies, a sweatshirt and grubby socks, into a corner. The utensils in his box went into Fritz's locker and the empty box he shoved under the bed. As he exited the cell he grabbed the cardboard box Fritz had left at the door, neatly folded sheets and blankets balanced on top. They were now his, to replace the ones he left in Fritz's cell.

The dog handlers had failed to locate Fritz's escape path outside the prison because of a simple ploy. Cleverly duped by Fritz and his friend, they searched for the wrong scent!

+ + + +

Fritz knew he had to be in position to see John's window by seven forty-eight to watch for the shirt signal. Not one minute later. Which was early for the garden gang's movement, but better early than too late. Time is relative under pressure and it is impossible to calculate it accurately. However, Fritz did carry a solution.

Contraband in prison is a never-ending circle of wits involving acquisition and confiscation. A screw received eight times the value to smuggle in a tiny wristwatch the size of a five-cent piece, without the band. But when I got it, knowing the exact time every minute of the night, the long prison hours drove me mad! I finally gave it to Fritz a month later thinking he might find a better use for it. Which he did, holding it in the dark where he hid, watching the radium-tipped minute hand creep round the dial towards the ten.

Fritz told me his initial move, stepping out into the open and walking back towards A-division in morning sunlight, had him feeling vulnerable and felt harder to do than what followed afterwards. Screws were rushing about to get to their assigned work places, while he had to appear as though he were on a mission carrying a box headed somewhere with a purpose. Can you imagine the thumping of his heart, and how exposed he felt, psyching up to what was yet to come?

The moment the roofline of B-division came into view and the last few windows at the top appeared, he faltered. No shirt in sight. He couldn't loiter and he couldn't return. Fritz did the only thing he could do in that kind of situation: he continued walking slowly until he saw clearly on his left the scaffolding behind the cyclone-wire fence that defined no-man's-land and stopped in worried doubt. A few more steps and he would become visible to the tower on his right. He took a hurried glance at the watch-face to get the time: seven fifty-three. What to do?

A grey prison shirt fluttering from a B-division window made the decision for him. Engaging an ability very few ordinary individuals have, he switched to an alter-ego I have seen him do many times. Soldiers who have experienced battle have it, and I will concede that quite a few police have it too. Under extreme threat, I have been able to engage detachment too, but not on demand like Fritz could.

He placed the box on the ground and ran for a section of cyclone-wire fence below where the shirt fluttered, towards the scaffolding and breach visible in the wall above. No thought of the lethal threat in the tower entered his mind to deter him. The shirt above engendered the confidence to pull out the blanket strip tucked in his belt and allow it to unfurl as the fence approached.

With uncanny ease, Fritz later told me, it snagged the barbed wire above with his first attempt. Then with one solid tug, he dragged the wire down until it refused to collapse further. With hardly a twang from the taut wire, he ascended the piece of blanket to the top of the fence. Balanced there precariously on the squashed barbed wire, he lifted the piece of blanket and looped it over a pole in the fence which he used to descend halfway to the ground before letting go, falling the rest of the way into 'dead man' terrain with the strip of blanket held tight in one hand.

The scaffolding was as easy to climb as a ladder, which in a sense it was. Kneeling at the top looking over his shoulder, he could just see the fluttering shirt, signalling that all was still okay. He leaned across the wall between the loose bricks and stared down the other side – a daunting drop of probably six metres with long grass below. Maintaining his cold mental state but as quick as a flash, Fritz wrapped the blanket around his arms from elbows to wrists until they were virtually wound together cocooned in blanket for the feat to follow.

He turned and crawled backwards. Hanging from the wall like a bat, mentally unable to let go and crash to the ground below, he closed his eyes and focused on the consequences of failure . . . his fingers relaxed and down the wall, he instantly fell.

If not for the protection of the blanket, his forearms would have been a bleeding mess, shredded by the weathered bluestone in the two seconds it took to reach the ground as the friction of the blanket slowed his velocity. The sudden impact of hitting the ground snapped his left knee sickeningly into the wall as he folded in pain to lay semi-stunned in dewy grass. It took all his willpower to raise himself up, ignoring the pain to get moving again.

With a throbbing knee injury that later troubled him for weeks, Fritz limped away from the wall, subduing the pain, towards the high perimeter fence, the last obstacle still blocking his freedom. A hundred metres of prison property to cover and if any of the tower guards spotted him he could still be lawfully shot. But he gambled that all watched inwards now that Yatala had come to life and hundreds of prisoners were on the move. Blanket clutched to his chest with one hand, Fritz never took a backward look.

He lay alongside the security fence in a furrow of ground where weather had eroded some of the soil from around the buried wire. Covered by the scrap of blanket and using a rusted sardine can sighted and gathered up in passing, Fritz scraped away the hard earth. The piece of tin he used was a godsend; he acknowledged that without it his bare hands alone could not have done the job. With barely enough soil removed, and the sun high in the sky, Fritz finally squeezed under the fence and gained his freedom.

16
DREAMIN'

Police lock-up in central Victoria

IF WISHES WERE CARS, BEGGARS WOULD DRIVE

"Have you been watching the news, Bob?" were the first words I heard when I picked up the phone to find out who was calling me at midnight. No need to ask who it was at the other end; referring to me as Bob (a false name used by me that only a few knew) and the distinctive accent identified him as a friend.

"Yeah," I answered, no longer feeling sleepy. "What about it, Leo?" my pulse quickening. I had automatically slipped into using his alias as well. It had to be either an emergency, or crime related. Leo did not make social calls.

"You must come to Brisbane tomorrow," he stated. No ifs, or buts, or how's your health. His was a constantly whirling mind, like a roller-coaster and the ghost-train rolled into one only much scarier.

"I'm locked in here, mate, on bail," I replied, thinking he had forgotten that I was reporting twice daily to a police station, the strictest bail conditions the court could impose in my case. "Have you overlooked that little fact?"

His next statement made my pulse race. "A mill each, Joe," he whispered down the phone-line, forgetting that he had just used my real name! It felt awesome hearing him say a million dollars. In the past when making a rough estimate of a job's take he unerringly guestimated within a thousand dollars of the final count. And I had no reason to doubt his nose for money now.

"I can't do it, mate," was my instant reflex response. I was finished with crime, or at least I thought I was, until I heard the dream number every crook is ready to come out of retirement for. But my gut feeling, the gut of a gambler, screamed, 'Yes, yes!'

He didn't hesitate to consider my predicament when replying, nor did he pull his punches. "Fuck that, Joe. You owe me big time." He had saved my life once and my freedom a few times too. But the bottom line here, and he knew it, was that I had promised him years before that if ever the shit hit the fan, or he needed the favour returned, I would be there for him. He knew my principles bound me to keep my word.

"What is it?" I asked, not expecting him to blurt it out over the phone but to at least hint at what it was. The phone went silent, but I knew Leo was still there. He was thinking up an answer to give without actually saying anything incriminating.

"We will need Bruce to help us," he finally said. "And you don't need to bring any stuff." I knew instantly that he meant drugs of some kind, and that the crime was a walk-up start. Bruce was in prison serving five years for dealing. He dealt in kilos, not ounces and grams. Drugs then were mostly organic and not chemical and no one could have envisaged the scourge they are now. I had no concept back in the late 80s of the dreadful consequences of illicit drugs. All I saw was the immediate potential of gaining a bucket of money. But the idea of walking into some place and picking up the equivalent of a million dollars each without the use of violence, or even tools needed, made me think I had heard it wrong.

"Are you tooled up?" I queried, thinking he already had every tool needed. How a rip-off of that magnitude could be carried out without confrontation or destruction was beyond me at that moment. "I have entry," was his hoarse reply.

I should have known that cunning and stealth was at the heart of it with Leo involved. Not violent by nature (whereas I am) made him a far more capable criminal, because he constantly thought outside the box. He obviously had keys or some other guaranteed way in. I lost count of the times he found easy access into premises, and often even into locked safes, by being observant and simply taking advantage of his victims' negligence. And then I recalled the televised newscast Leo had alluded to at the start of our phone conversation.

According to the television reporter, an overseas schooner smuggling drugs into Australia had been intercepted and boarded by customs and police off the coast of central Queensland only the day before. Graphic footage showed the schooner being tied up at a deepwater jetty, with five dejected-looking handcuffed men being bustled off the vessel and hastily pushed into waiting police vehicles. A half dozen or so plastic-wrapped and gaffer-taped packages were quickly loaded into a Hertz rental truck, the confiscated drugs presumably, and whisked away to an undisclosed destination. Suspecting where they may have taken it and guessing now what Leo was contemplating, typical of an inveterate gambler,

I stepped off the plank into the unknown, excited.

Without applying the heavy thought a serious crime like this warranted, or even considering how it would impact on my future life, my answer consisted of just two words: "When and where?"

+ + + +

Adelaide airport hummed with activity. It seemed that everyone booked on a flight, except me, had someone in the departure terminal wishing them well and *bon voyage*. I stood alone near a row of empty seats, too nervous to sit, watching a matronly woman behind a desk stare into a console while she tapped with her fingers at a keyboard. She gave it her full attention for ten minutes until finally she looked my way and beckoned me over.

The task I had given her had been a challenge, and I am sure she bumped a passenger or two out of their seats for me. Fifteen minutes earlier I had spun a tale to her that I had to be in Rockhampton before 6 pm. that evening to seal an important deal. After a thorough search by her of the available seats, she told me that it could only be done after 10 pm, no earlier. But I know there are always flight cancellations, delayed arrivals, and other unforeseen changes which travellers accept and go along with even though they might grumble. I gave her a financial inducement for one of those options to occur.

"There is no point in paying, sir," she said as I commenced placing money on the counter. "I can't put you on a flight before ten."

"That's okay," I responded as I pushed five $50 notes towards her (in 2013, equivalent to $1000). "When you find me a seat, I don't expect any change." I strolled away without looking left or right, towards the coffee shop nearby. She didn't call me back.

Approaching the counter, her smile told me everything. Her

words confirmed it. "I have two flights logged, sir. One is direct to Brisbane at three-thirty this afternoon, and a connecting flight with another airline to Rockhampton. Is that suitable, sir?"

I grabbed at it verbally, "Yes." And while waiting for the ticket to be printed out I calculated the time-frame. It suited me better than expected; all I had to do now was leave a message for Leo at his contact number, giving my arrival time at Rocky.

My partner worried when I told her that I would not be home that night, but was satisfied with my story of staying overnight with Eugene, a friend who lived in Gumeracha, an outlying town north-east of Adelaide. The strict bail conditions set by the court where I was opposing an application by the Victorian Parole Board to extradite me to Victoria made it compulsory that I report twice daily, once in every twelve hours, but those seemingly strict conditions were easily circumvented once I had sufficient incentive to think about it.

Before coming to the airport I had reported to the Holden Hill police station where I signed the Bail Book as required; it meant that I was now covered until midnight. My next report could be as late as noon the next day before my bail could be forfeited, giving me twenty hours of unrestricted movement if I had the balls to ignore the court order restricting me to Adelaide risking imprisonment, casting my fate to the wind and leave the state anonymously.

Throughout the previous twelve months I had complied with the bail order without complaint nor made any attempt to have it reduced, knowing that by leaving it unchallenged I appeared to have coped with the encumbrance well, never thinking that I would one day abuse it. How often does a million dollar enticement fall in your lap?!

With an overnight bag under my head as a pillow, I stretched out on the airport seats to rest. No way could I sleep hyped up the way I felt, knowing that rest was better than pacing the terminal. I knew Leo would have pills to keep me awake when next we met. Not for a moment during that waiting period did I entertain thoughts of failure. My visions constantly dipped and soared – a million dollars – seeking mental answers to questions my mind had not yet formed.

+ + + +

The one and a half hour flight to Brisbane was uneventful, but the forty minute wait I had to endure sitting immobile in the bustling international airport terminal waiting for the connecting leg to Rockhampton eroded my confidence. Even though I travelled under a false name, I had suddenly become aware of the many surveillance cameras scattered throughout the airport. Their existence had me on edge knowing they were recording my every move and, if reviewed by inquisitive police, could later be used as condemning evidence in court.

The risk I was taking blatantly disobeying a court order, and the seriousness of the crime we were contemplating slowly drew my thoughts inward to the daunting possibility of my freedom lost, and long imprisonment if caught. But, true to my gamblers temperament (more aptly a Masada complex) I shrugged it off, subduing my subversive thoughts and forged on, going with my gut, believing like I did in 1975 when the 1974 Melbourne Cup winner Think Big did it back-to-back at 33/1. I bet $100 on him, contrary to all the advice given by my 'expert' racing friends, and won big that day.

Finally the call I had been sweating on: "Passengers boarding Rockhampton, flight number . . ."

+ + + +

At the Rocky terminal I walked straight for the exit door without even bothering to look around for Leo. He would either be outside waiting, or still on the road heading for me. He never put his face on camera unnecessarily. And sure enough, as I got a full view of the passenger pick-up rank I saw Leo's kombi van, in amongst similarly parked vehicles, waiting for me.

"Good for coming, Joe," was Leo's greeting as we shook hands. I settled into the passenger seat and belted up as he negotiated the airport exit, anxious to begin the long drive north, up the Bruce highway to our final destination. "This one is big and very dangerous too," he said. "They have it at the cop shop."

"Yeah, that's what I figured. Is it coke?" I asked. The news reporter said the boat had been tracked across the Pacific Ocean by satellite from Chile, but he never said what substance it smuggled.

"Sure, cocaine. Will Bruce be able to sell it for us from inside?" he queried, and by the look on his face, worried that Bruce would be unable to help. Like me, he knew next-to-nothing about the machinations within the burgeoning drug scene.

"Don't worry it," I said. "Bruce is one of the very few who can reach out to his contacts and get things done. Besides, when it comes off he's got you and me to rely on to do his running around."

I asked a question that burned in me for an answer: "How do we get in?"

"I have keys, Joe. Five years ago I found an old set when searching for their money-book." What was not commonly known is that police were often used to escort local payrolls and bank deposits, and that required a book to keep track of the dates and premises, even listing the names of the officers assigned to the escort. Leo called it a 'money book' for obvious reasons and would use the information to backtrack and find the business where the cash originated.

"Where are the keys now?" I queried. I wanted to be sure we really did have a guaranteed entry. No way did I want to risk my neck breaking into a 24/7 police station using tools. It could be done – Leo has proven that – but not by yours truly!

"I have them here," he said. Reaching into a door pocket he promptly produced a bank-bag filled with more than just keys. The bag bulged as though it were full of money. He handed it to me saying, "I had them hidden in my garden. They are a bit rusty, Joe."

What an understatement that was! On the ring of keys I pulled out, two of them were aluminium alloy and had been half eaten away by corrosion. A third one of a similar type but made of brass was so twisted out of shape it should have broken. Half-a-dozen other keys were of similar size and fortunately all were in good condition, and two large badly rusted black-iron keys I instantly recognised were for the cell-block. "These are stuffed!" I blurted out, shaking the keys. "Do you know which key opens what?" I was disappointed by the amateurish attempt Leo had made of cleaning them up. In the bottom of the bag sat a set of professional locksmith files rolled in canvas, with sheets of various grades of emery paper torn into quarters, and a tattered T-shirt stuffed on top.

Forced to ignore the shoulder shrug he nonchalantly gave in answer, I located the largest ward-file in the kit and commenced removing rust from the grooves inside the black-iron keys. Leo figured the drugs would be secured in a cell, so first things first. This particular police station had its cell-block built separate, outside the main building, making it vulnerable to a direct attack.

+ + + +

With the van parked on the southern outskirts of town, pulled in out of sight under a massive Morton Bay fig growing in a truck lay-by on the side of the highway, Leo quickly set about preparing a hot meal for us both while I went through his tool box selecting a few tools in the worst event that the keys failed to fit.

An earlier drive-by of the police station confirmed Leo's conclusion. The two-storey building blazed with light like a cruise liner docked in a Pacific Island port for the night. Every window in the complex shone brightly, and twenty vehicles or so were parked inside as well as more out on the curb. Just seeing it did enough to make my heart palpitate knowing all the guns and testosterone-driven authority in there could blast us to oblivion if they detected what was to come.

"After ten, one shift will be gone," Leo confidently asserted. "By then, we will be out the back watching," he added. "And I bet they won't keep the prisoners here."

I agreed with him about the imminent future of the captured boat crew. Beyond a doubt, after their interrogation finished, because of their high profile crime they would be swiftly transported to Rockhampton Prison, not held for any length of time in a local police lock-up. Knowing that fact was a valuable advantage and our only concern was that the drugs might get relocated at the same time. Therefore, a position to watch from had to be perfect to see what each enforcement group involved in the arrest did and to observe what happened as they gradually returned to their normal operations. We were prepared to continue the surveillance if they failed to scale down this night. I would return to Adelaide for the morning bail report and then in the afternoon, following my second report for the day, again fly across to finish the job. A lot of risk involved, but it could be done.

Carrying a flat pry-bar and a torch, I handed Leo his two-way as we set out together in the dark heading cross-country through farm properties towards our destination. On the walk we rehearsed our two-way code: the use of voice over the airwaves is a no-no. In any big town the likelihood of other users picking us up was high. Besides, if your mind is clear and your objectives are focused, conversation on a job is generally generated by nerves and therefore superfluous.

Our two-way set had a weak range and lacked multiple channels, but made up for its deficiencies by having ear-pieces and a powerful contact beeper used to alert the other to power-up their set when a call was incoming. Only we never make the call. One buzz meant *stop and listen,* two buzzes indicated *safe or begin,* three buzzes said *danger,* and four meant *retreat now.* If a shot was heard, the shit had hit the fan!

+ + + +

At the rear of a motel near its back fence, concealed within a thicket of Japanese bamboo and short ornamental palms, we watched the police building gradually downgrade its lighting system as the hour approached midnight. More than half of the vehicles had already departed by the time we were in position, and more drove away into the night until eventually only a few cars remained at the rear. I had become comfortable hiding there in deep shadow, a warm night, not overly worried by what lay ahead . . . until Leo spoke.

"We must do it soon, Bob (using my 'job' name in case he was overheard). The moon will rise at two." He knew all about that kind of shit; once he set his mind to a job he could have told you what time the tide came in at Perth if it were relevant.

Standing with the pry-bar in hand, my stomach suddenly became very fluttery and I even felt my face flush. Taking on the police was not what brought it on – there were a few unprincipled criminals I have crossed swords with who had bothered me far more – no, it was the fact that crime had always excited me until then, realising in that moment of epiphany that I had finally put my addiction to rest.

To pull out now was not an option because of my commitment to Leo, but I knew when standing there win, lose, or draw, one way or the other this would conclude my run as a career criminal. Luckily, before I broke the golden rule of silence by babbling to cover my drear doubts, Leo jumped the fence into a long carport and sped off dipping in and out of shadow to abruptly disappear around the brightly lit rear of the station to where I knew the cell-block was located. Tall coconut palms and a few fern bushes grew randomly in the roughly mowed grassed area behind the building.

For five minutes I watched the corner of the building where I expected to see Leo reappear, concentrating totally on his point of disappearance rather than scan the windows as I should have been. A sudden movement in one of the few lit windows on the floor above snapped my eyes towards it. A man and a woman filled the frame staring through the glass directly at me!

I froze, but my thoughts raced: *Could we have already been detected?* And as I thought *'Should I warn Leo',* he unexpectedly came into sight as he turned the corner of the building. I jabbed at the button on my two-way, *one – two – three* and Leo stopped instantly, pressing his back against the wall, directly below the two detectives above. Because of the distance I could view both scenes, so when the two withdrew with the woman talking silently and the man nodding, I intuitively knew it was still okay. I buzzed, twice, to tell him that it was now safe.

He unfroze and faced me, to slowly tap his head twice: *come to me*. It made me instantly feel fluttery in the stomach. Not giving the nerves time to work on my doubts, I clambered over the fence and ran directly to him. With only metres between us he peered around the building in the direction he had appeared from, and slipped out of sight. It was expected that I follow him.

The rear of the building was brightly lit, more than I expected, compared to the side I had been watching. Exposed like a hare in headlights, Leo raced to the bluestone wall of the cell-block twenty metres from me. I stopped instead of blindly following, with my back pressed against the brick wall breathing deeply, to wait for an all-clear signal from Leo for the windows above. A bright arc-light shone over the entrance of the cell-block lighting up everything around it.

He buzzed me twice, adding emphasis by tapping his head, *come to me*. In total trust, I plunged into the light and sped to him. Behind the cells in a tiny swathe of shadow we pushed our backs hard against the bluestone blocks to get our breath back. After a careful look by Leo around the other side, he again tapped his head indicating that I should edge up close to him.

"From over there," he whispered, pointing towards a large mango tree hanging over the fence from the adjoining property, "you can watch for me." He meant that I would be his eyes and ears while he worked blind at the front of the cell-block. Taking one long glance at the few lit windows I could see from where I stood to confirm no one watched, I loped to the beckoning shrubbery.

With my upper body pressed hard against a wooden fence, I again felt relatively safe as I peered through the leafy branches to scan the entire rear and up one side of the building. Satisfied that a few muffled sounds I could hear coming from within the building were normal, I signalled Leo to go: *one – two*.

Down the side of the cell-block he hurried, hugging the wall, and then stepped around the corner out of sight at the front into the breezeway. Within two minutes of watchful waiting the strain had me feeling anxious. And by five minutes my inner misgivings about Leo had run riot and I was beginning to feel panicky. I cautioned myself to slow down mentally, knowing that time was being lengthened by nervous worry. My breathing was fast and shallow, so I drew deeper breaths to calm my mind and started a slow count: one ... two ... three ...

The back door of the building swung open! Two people dressed in blue casually stepped out. In a blast of sensory input everything slowed down, my mind accelerated, totally focused – *one, two, three, four* presses of the button – totally destroying any calm I may have had.

+ + + +

Peering through the Judas hole of the locked door of a cell, Leo froze to the sound of the ear-buds' urgent message: then, like a wolf detecting danger he sprinted towards the deepest end of the short passage in the cell-block. The security light at the entrance to the building cast deep zebra-like shadows through the heavily barred gate securing the entrance. Five cell doors, two each side of the wide passage, with the fifth door ajar in the end wall. Leo eased it open just enough to squeeze through. With a gaze of total concentration, he watched through the gap in the doorframe for movement in the shadows ... and waited.

+ + + +

As emotionally heightened as the circumstance was, I stayed in control for Leo, reading the situation as it rapidly unfolded. They each wore a blue uniform which had triggered my fright, but the shoulder insignia was wrong for police – maybe customs? – and by the time they had taken the four or five steps it took for them to turn away from the door and disappear from sight, hidden by the cell-block, I knew they would not enter the cells without a cop present. *One, two, three,* I buzzed Leo, to let him know that it was less serious. I willed them to keep walking.

+ + + +

Leo raised his arms above his head to ease the obvious tension he had been under; the triple buzz in his ear had reassured him. But still he remained in the cell waiting for the all-clear signal before resuming his search. The cell he stood in was empty except for a collapsed pile of blankets, and the two cells at the front each held a lone Aboriginal prisoner. Only the cells each side of him remained unknown.

+ + + +

When the two in blue reappeared I watched as they headed away from me towards the carport Leo and I had hidden behind earlier. A small car sat at the end of it next to the fence; one I had not even registered as being there!

I depressed the button twice to let Leo know it was *safe or begin*, so he could continue whatever it was he had been doing. I exercised my feet, as well as bent my knees, to ease the ache in my legs I was experiencing for having stood immobile for so long in the same place. Only one solitary light now remained aglow in a rear window above the back entrance of the police building and I suspected that it was left on for a passageway or a stairwell.

A need to know was again creeping into my mind . . . *Buzz, buzz;* my thoughts instantly focused as the bud in my ear resonated. Leo had finished and was asking if it was okay to come out. I gave him a quick two back as an all-clear signal.

Out of sight at the front of the cell-block, I imagined him unlocking the gate to quickly exit the building; then standing outside under the security light, taking the risk of being spotted to carefully relock the gate before stepping into shadow at the corner of the block.

He appeared in stark silhouette and ran like a sprinter directly towards me. I made room for him behind the branches by hastily moving left and indicating with my right hand waving down low where he would see it in the light. He squirmed in under the branches and pushed up beside me, breathing deeply like someone who had just run a marathon.

"In there are two local boys," Leo whispered as soon as he got his breath back. "No packages." I felt my heart drop and stomach burn, disappointed, an immediate let-down of hope.

"I must go inside." He said it so calmly, yet nevertheless my heart pulsed with anxiety even though I knew it would be him and not me making that perilous entry.

I agreed with him, tempted to say the obvious but knowing anything said by me now would be gratuitous. Instead, I stated a relieved, "Best of luck, mate." And honestly added, "I don't think I'd be up to it."

He stifled a laugh: Leo excelled at this cat-and-mouse game, and he knew it. We agreed to stand down until three in the morning – the best time to sneak in – two hours away. The place behind the fence where the tree grew was a private residence, and rather than risk a dog barking or being reported lurking in someone's backyard, we took the harder option of returning to the motel's rear.

+ + + +

It was almost three-thirty when the local paddy wagon, which had sat parked at the front of the police station for the last hour, finally drove away on patrol with two uniforms in the front. Ten minutes earlier, we had watched two detectives accompanied by a uniformed constable enter the cell-block and return into the building with two handcuffed prisoners. The detectives soon left with both prisoners in an unmarked sedan. With the building seemingly empty of police, now was the best opportunity Leo had of entering undetected to conduct a sly search; and if detected by the lone station keeper he stood the best chance of getting away.

The thought of escalating to the building, after not finding the drugs in the cell-block as we had hoped, set my nerves jumping now that it was about to happen. Being a direct-action individual, Leo made no issue of the audacious risk he was undertaking other than to give me a brief outline of what he would do if discovered inside; my role continued as nit-keeper with an added aspect of covering his arse if he emerged with a uniform in hot pursuit.

The time spent waiting had not been wasted. We had worked for thirty minutes in the deep shadows cast by the security lights, stringing barely visible shark-line at chest height from the cell-block to a coconut tree; and the same again from where I would watch in hiding from under the overhanging mango tree to the rear fence; and two more taut lines between a few posts of the carport and out to nearby bushes. If Leo was forced to exit at speed he knew exactly where *not to run* and if his pursuer thought they were clever enough to cut him off by taking a shorter route than the zigzag one Leo ran they would be smacked to the ground before they could even comprehend what had befallen them. But if forced through unforeseen circumstances to exit from the front into the main street then he was on his own, and if not shot, then capture was very likely. I took possession of the keys to the cell-block just in case of that unlikely eventuality.

"Bob, I must go now before I lose my nerves," Leo agitatedly whispered. He sped towards the rear door without further comment, inserting his ear-bud as he ran. Taken by surprise, I rushed to my vantage point and dived in under the branches. No sooner had I caught sight of Leo, and he was running back towards me!

Someone must be coming out dominated my thoughts. I willed Leo to run faster while I stared at the door waiting for a cop to exit. If spotted and a shout went up, I intended to stay exactly where I was. When Leo eluded them he would take full advantage of the kerfuffle and depleted staff, like a cunning fox that outwits its hunters, to return and raid the unguarded hen-house.

He dived in under the concealing branches next to me. "What the fuck!" I exclaimed in surprised shock, prepared to flee with my eyes still glued to the lit rear entrance. Yet no one emerged in the following few moments that ticked by.

As I calmed myself, Leo explained his actions in a panted rush of words. "The door is fuckin' locked! You must give me back the keys!" He nudged me hard with his arm to emphasise his demand. As quick as possible I removed the two large cell keys from the ring and palmed him the remaining few. The relief I felt of him not being pursued was outweighed by my worry that the keys he held were not standard door keys. Because of previous experience with police arrogance, we had wrongly believed that the rear door of the building might not be locked.

Without indicating his intention, Leo again sped towards the lit doorway while I tensed up expecting the worst, praying for him not to be sprung. His hunched back concealed what he did with the keys, but the time he took was far too long if any of them had worked. I surmised he was retrying them again, which meant the lock was at least compatible and of similar vintage as the keys. I hoped for success, while simultaneously envisaging failure in all of its many guises.

He disappeared! As nimble as a ninja assassin he had opened the door and closed it behind him in one fluid movement. Like a conjuror's smoke trick, Leo vanished into the building's interior, out of the fry-pan and possibly into the fire. I worried for him.

+ + + +

Unhesitant, Leo sped across the linoleum floor for the stairwell to the level above. Relying on the knowledge of years before when he had originally acquired the keys, he knew that detective squads used the top floor. His search would begin there.

Wraithlike, with torch in hand, he nipped in and out of each dark office as he encountered them, confirming at a glance or the quick opening of a cupboard that the boxes he sought were not stored within. Only two doors had been locked and he now stood before one of them. A simple mortise-lock barred his way.

Leo had come prepared: he carried a variety of bump-keys, a strip of flexible celluloid, and a 60's hubcap remover. Applying the easiest method first and the one most likely to work, he slipped the celluloid strip into the gap between the door and the jamb and vigorously wiggled it forward until it touched the tongue of the lock. A forceful forward push of the plastic, a gentle nudge, and the door opened inwards. It was an interrogation room devoid even of furniture, probably used to soften up an accused before the serious questioning actually began. Leo moved along to the next locked door.

After three failed attempts to slip the lock (this one had a square tongue) he desisted and produced his ring of bumper keys. Most internal locks are inferior to external locks (simple economics) so Leo inserted a key and tapped away at it with the rubber-dipped handle of the small lever he carried, confident that the sound would not be heard even though he knew a uniform manned the twenty-four hour desk near the entrance on the floor below. Fifty taps later he stopped, frustrated that it had not yet opened, tempted to resort to the lever and force the door. But wisdom prevailed; if the door was damaged without the certainty of the boxes being in there then a simple check by a bored copper doing his rounds would foil our game.

Knowing he lacked a second bumper to fit that make of lock, resigned,

Leo reinserted the one he'd been using and again tapped away. Within a minute of repetitive strikes the pins were finally jumped collectively and the key turned.

One long sweep of the torch-beam revealed why the room had been locked: from floor to ceiling around the walls and piled high on two desks pushed together, were a clutter of boxes. Though not the ones he hoped for after a hastily carried-out search dashed his first impression. These boxes were filled with old ledgers and police reports, office material, case evidence, court papers and a miscellany of other stuff Leo considered worthless.

✚ ✚ ✚ ✚

Nit-keeping for Leo while he moved about upstairs – the windows revealed muted light as he searched the rooms on my side of the building – caused waves of anxiety in me as time crawled by. The moon's gradual appearance overhead turned the yard from dark shadows to silver, and the shark-lines strung around flickered like strands of wet spider web, in and out of vision as the shadows changed, cast by the moving clouds above. I didn't enjoy being exposed by the moonlight, nor the uncomfortable feeling of exposure it caused.

A car suddenly pulled into the side of the building, giving me such a fright as its headlights lit the wall and the grass all the way to where I stood concealed against the fence under the branches, my legs from the knees down clearly visible in the stark light. My heart raced even though I knew at that range a person would need to look specifically for legs to actually spot them. Nevertheless I kept my wits, my stomach churning, not yet prepared to buzz an early warning to Leo of the threat their arrival posed for him once they entered the building.

The headlights blinked out, plunging the area back into darkness. I quickly pressed the call button three times, *danger*. The crump of two doors being slammed momentarily panicked me, but the adrenalin rush released me from my frozen state. Unwisely I had stared at the headlights for too long and all I could now see, no matter how hard I squinted and tried, were flashes of light burnt into my retinas, my night vision destroyed. Not knowing whether the occupants of the car were headed for the front door, or in my direction towards the rear entry, I forced myself to stay focused. Leo's safety depended on me. If I buzzed him now to get out of there, and I tipped it wrong, he could exit at the rear directly into them.

Like the negative of a photograph, the headlights of a passing car silhouetted a human shape just as it disappeared from view towards the front door! Four times I pressed the button, *retreat now*. And I sent another four, just to be sure he got them and to impress the urgency of it on Leo.

+ + + +

The cop sitting at the front desk tapping away at a typewriter had no idea that he had been watched so intently from the sideline. In response to three buzzes, Leo rapidly crawled out of a room he had been in to where he now lay curled up on the linoleum floor beside a desk with barely enough concealment to hide behind. Three buzzes meant a threat was imminent from outside; but which direction would it come from? Front or back? His ear-bud beeped four times, solving the dilemma for him. Get out now! And that meant the rear door. Otherwise the signal to retreat would not have been sent.

KNOCK, KNOCK, KNOCK! *Knuckles rapped on the front door. Leo froze, but only for a moment. At the sound of a chair being hastily vacated by the constable at the front in hurried response to the unexpected knocking, Leo made his move. Any hesitation now and the game would end in tears.*

Like a lizard slithering on sand, he scarpered on his belly through the open doorway into the room he had just vacated. With voices in greeting heard behind him he leapt up and raced through an exit – a lunchroom with two entries – back into the passage with the locked rear door of the building at the end beckoning him.

+ + + +

My heart thumped, as though it were me in there and not Leo. *Where is he?* my thoughts repeated over and over like a chant: *Where is he?* I stared at the door, willing it to fly open, *Where is he?*

I must have blinked or glanced away for a moment, but incredibly when I looked again he stood there exposed in the harsh security lighting of the cell-block with his arms spread wide in a Homer Simpson 'What the – !' gesture indicating his anxiety for the all-clear signal that it was safe to leave the cover of the building. I gave him two.

In a swift few seconds he reached me and dived in under the branches. Though concealed as we were, I foolishly believed for a moment that if someone emerged and listened quietly we'd be detected for certain by the combined sounds of his stentorian breathing and my hammering heart.

While he regained his breath, I noted that a light came on in the rear section of the building. On the ground floor first, followed a minute or two later by one coming on in an office above. Knowing sunrise was less than two hours away I dejectedly withdrew to the relative safety of the motel garden, but not before releasing all of the shark-line snares we had set, leaving them to innocuously hang ready to be reset the next night. We were coming back to finish it.

Travelling through the paddocks back to our transport, Leo painted a vivid word picture of what he had discovered inside and how he had gone about it. I listened closely to his description. Except for two locked rooms at the front of the building where the station keeper sat, every other room in the complex had been cursorily searched. Crawling through an office area using desks for concealment to reach a section at the front where cabinets against the front wall concealed him, Leo had been able to stand and look across to minutely study both doors. His reasoning made me agree with him that one particular room contained the goods we were after.

Being centrally located it lacked a window and had a quality mortise-lock in the door, making it the most secure room in the building. But the more telling fact confirming it for us was that the door had been recently fitted with a large new padlock and bolt. It indicated that someone in charge did not implicitly trust his staff and wanted singular control over the contents in that room.

The risks taken to get us this close to achieving the dream of a million dollars, with only a desk-cop and a locked door between us were not going to be wasted by running away defeated. Where there is a will, there is *always* a way.

In Leo's van headed back down the highway towards Rockhampton airport, we tossed around a variety of ideas. Leo urged me to stay with him and rotate daylight surveillance of the place, but I was adamant that while my bail still existed I would do my utmost to maintain it by returning to Adelaide and sign in before midday to prevent an arrest warrant being issued. He accepted that he had to continue the surveillance alone and agreed to pick me up that evening after my flight back to Rocky.

I had not realised how much the episode stressed my nerves until Leo said I must come up with a diversion to draw the cop out of the station and it had to work for at least eight to ten minutes. My response was weak: "I'll need to think it through on the plane back to Adelaide." I had mentally gone blank.

I diverted him by asking what he planned on doing to get the packages. "A rubber wedge under the front door to stop entry," Leo explained. "It opens in and I'll use a crowbar to smash the lock." He stated triumphantly, "That *always* works!"

I cringed at the old memories his assertion stirred, recalling the noise and destruction he had caused doing just that on a few other jobs we had done together. I tried to temporise his action a bit by saying that a jemmy-bar might be better . . . but he talked over me.

"No, Joe. It'll be fire-wood in a few hits. And then you must be there to take two boxes each." I nodded my head, frustrated but agreeing to the inevitable, knowing that I couldn't fault his logic. He then asked the very same question I was thinking: "Is cocaine heavy?"

While he enthused over what lay ahead, I listened in a drowsy state, until the lights of Rocky were gradually revealed on the horizon. With the rising sun almost blinding us, Leo drove east to the airport and pulled in to drop me off. The terminal hummed with activity as the first flight of the day was loading for Brisbane, and I rushed to the desk in an attempt to get aboard. Too late, they said, the plane was full, and the next flight to Brisbane was not until noon. The following flight out of there was Sydney-bound.

Two hours later the plane I dozed in woke me as it began its descent over the central New South Wales coast. I figured that a few early business flights from Sydney to Adelaide were a certainty and would get me over there long before noon and my bail's expiry hour.

The long flight to Adelaide was therapeutic: I slept most of the way. With an hour to spare after landing, I showered in the airport terminal and then organised return flights to Rockhampton. After that, I cruised in a taxi to Holden Hill police station to sign the Bail Book just before noon. And later in muted sunshine, stretched out on a park bench not far from there, sleep embraced me till two in the afternoon.

I again entered the Holden Hill police station and requested to sign the Bail Book – the afternoon shift had taken over so a different sergeant manned the desk – which now covered me through to midnight and beyond. I called for a taxi to take me direct to the anonymity of Hindmarsh Square. I still had some tactical thinking to do, and the best place to do it was strolling in the bustling centre of Adelaide.

Late that afternoon, while waiting in a queue at the airport to reach the bookings desk to confirm my flights, I was surprised to see a friend enter the terminal. My first instinct was to wave and call Andrew over and ask where he was off to, but quickly quelled that urge as I realised he would ask the same question of me! Putting the issue of trust aside, the gravity of the criminal venture embarked upon prevented me from telling anyone anything.

I turned side on and edged closer to a matronly woman ahead of me in the line so that I could watch partly hidden and observe what Andrew did. He gazed around peering intently at the throng of bustling people in the terminal, instead of scanning the overhead flight boards as I would have expected if he were intending to take a flight out of there. His roving eyes passed over me twice before I came to a worrying conclusion: he was definitely searching for someone! And I instinctively thought that maybe it was me . . .

When his back faced my direction, I quickly ducked out of the line and joined a family of travellers who had just entered the terminal. As he turned and checked the group I hailed him as though I had entered with them and was surprised to see him there. After greeting each other warmly, I suggested that we get a coffee.

"Don't tell me your business has picked up so much that you need to travel interstate for new customers," I quizzed Andrew after sitting with our drinks at a small table, half joking so as not to let on that I had watched him search.

"Nah, mate, no. I've got a message from your mate in Rockhampton," he bluntly stated. His words unnerved me and my stomach went cold. Something serious must have happened, I thought, for Leo to take the drastic step of using my emergency contact number which was Andrew's. I nodded for him to continue, expecting the worst, to hear that Leo had been arrested and now needed my help. Luckily, I still carried the two cell-block keys.

Andrew delivered the message verbatim: "Tell Joe to drag the chain. The birds have slipped the noose." Shaking his head with amusement, Andrew added, "Whatever that means!" He looked at me expectantly.

Only Leo would mangle and mix metaphors to the point where they actually made sense! Obviously, unexpected events had occurred in Queensland. But I knew what the message meant: our venture had come to an end. All the risks taken had been for nothing.

Shooting the breeze with Andrew, while dodging the truth of why I was at the airport, I rode an emotional seesaw of relief that it was over, counteracted by conflicting emotions of regret and lost fortune. Provided no obvious evidence of our incursion existed back at Rockhampton, a crime had not been committed. My million dollar dream faded into oblivion.

+ + + +

Postscript:

Three weeks after receiving the 'stand down' message relayed via Andrew, Leo unexpectedly paid me an informative and profitable visit. The cocaine had been removed and transported in a police convoy to an unknown destination while I slept in a plane flying across New South Wales, headed for Adelaide. Leo had tailed them, but promptly withdrew within two kilometres when he realised that a vehicle was tracking him! Taking full advantage of the golden opportunity of the building being left unstaffed for a few hours, he sped back and rifled every desk in the police station, and came away with a swag of 'confiscated' bits and pieces that should *never* have been in a cop-shop. He only stayed a day in Adelaide, but when he departed I was wiser and, after selling the 'gifts' Leo gave me, three grand richer.

+ + + +

17
GAMMA RAYS

A chunk of Australian uranium ore

OBSERVATION TEACHES THROUGH TRUTH

Wandering the backblocks with a metal detector seeking whatever could be found has been an enjoyable pastime of mine, though I sometimes deviated with my detector from the correct course and used it for devious means. This tale weaves through both.

A metal detector does exactly what its name suggests: it detects metal. They have functions that discriminate common ferrous metals like iron and steel (magnetic) from non-ferrous metals such as gold and silver (not magnetic) which are fun to use if seeking old coins, something lost at the beach, or searching your own backyard. However, in the highly mineralised goldfields of Victoria they are next to useless.

Gold detectors on the other hand are designed to search specifically for gold in mineralised earth, and are capable of locating a piece of gold the size of a rice grain at twice the depth of a coin detector. However, away from the gold fields a dedicated gold detector is only marginally better at locating metal. There is so much interference from non-ferrous litter out there: aluminium ring-pulls, silver foil, brass bullet cases, copper wire, beer cans and shotgun pellets, ad infinitum. In some ways quite similar to stone-scatter left by Aborigines as they travelled the land, though magnitudes are different because the modern litter is intrusive and manufactured. With the slim chance of locating precious metal, though, a detector that can technically search deeper is better to own.

Therefore, I lashed out some real cash in the 90's and bought a proper gold detector: not that it ever located a gold nugget for me, but it did locate better quality trash. During my wanderings, usually wherever I stopped, the gold detector came with me, even if just for a roadside piss. The inbuilt functions and choice of various coils saved much of my time and effort, by eliminating the boring digging up of tin cans and sifting through soil hoping for gold, only to find a rusty nail or some such.

The reason the detector became attached to me is that more useful applications were found for it. Not intentionally, but gradually ideas grew through a few lucky finds. The first profitable incident had nothing to do with a quest for gold; it was car-keys lost by my next-door neighbour in his own backyard. While sweeping for them, I located a rusted tobacco tin filled with coins long ago secreted away — English florins — in the roots of a fig tree half way down the yard. Two perfectly good brass taps and a long length of lead pipe and the car keys of course had me on the right path of thinking, but not sufficiently yet to justify why I am relating this tale.

Fossicking across a paddock with nothing to show for my effort but a rusted axe-head found and thought worth keeping (it was a Plumb). The stump of a chimney showed where a farmhouse once stood. While resting there, I worked out where the back door must have been (farmers sat on their back step to remove or put on their dirty work boots), and sure enough, as soon as the detector got working in that area it gave a buzz. A tiny pearl-handled penknife turned up, rusted beyond use, and two silver coins: a sixpence, and a threepence. That is when the penny finally dropped, pun intended.

I developed a search strategy (not original, I later learned) to concentrate on settled areas where houses once stood, old worksites, church grounds, cemeteries, and country lanes. A little bit of research, and a few relaxing weekends spent prospecting likely areas, soon paid dividends. I never found gold of course, mostly just copper and brass fittings, lead strips, and many old horseshoes. However, my best find was inside a derelict cottage that I ran the detector over, and did that pay off big time!

The speaker on the detector buzzed when I swung the coil back and forth across the wall dividing the bedroom and kitchen (I only used sensitive headphones when searching foolishly in hope of gold). Because the buzz was strong and low-pitched, I figured it had to be a cast-iron water pipe from the rusted and collapsed tank still on its stand outside, to run water in to the kitchen sink. I went outside to confirm that I was right, hoping to at least find a brass spigot.

A short pipe was there, but it went directly through the wall of the kitchen to where a tap would have been over the sink. It passed nowhere near the bedroom wall. Intrigued, I went back inside the cottage to investigate.

An hour later, the effort spent demolishing the wall had spawned surprising fruit. A short-barrelled 303 Lee Enfield (cavalry) with its bolt and magazine inserted – no bullets – wrapped in a rat-gnawed blacksmith's leather apron along with a rusty Webley revolver in a Sam Brown holster that had seen better days. A coffee tin hidden with the find contained twenty rounds of corroded ammo for the Webley. But best of all, securely wrapped in a lightweight canvas satchel, I found a wooden box holding a Remington two-shot derringer in fair condition. The gold detector had finally paid for itself!

Torn between keeping my find a secret, to stop others getting in on my rort and boasting of how clever I was, only a few close friends heard of my luck. Bill was one of them. In fact, he eventually bought the 303 . . . but I am getting ahead of myself.

Before I had concluded telling him the whole story and the luck of my find, he asked to borrow the detector. I asked him why.

"I know a few old places to try," he responded. (The very thing I wanted to avoid!) However, knowing how shifty Bill was, I instantly suspected there was more to it than what he said.

"It's a bit complicated to use," I bullshitted to him. "But I'm happy to come with you and go sixty-forty your way with anything we find."

"Nah, mate; nope," he said with finality. "Show me how to work it; I don't want to put you out." Now I knew he was trying a con!

He was no Mister Nice Guy when it came to put money in his own pocket and would not hesitate to use someone to advance himself financially, even me. He had an idea – one held for a long time I suspected, to be so quick in asking – and I wanted to be in on it. "So, are you going to tell me the real reason?"

That forthright question got me nowhere, but a visit or two later, Bill put to me a new offer. A woman on a nearby property had come to him with a problem – he had been neighbourly with her father who died in a car accident three months earlier –

a problem she thought Bill could solve. Documentation needed to prove ownership of a shipping container and its contents stored on a factory site was missing, and she knew her father had kept his private papers in a cash box stashed somewhere on her property. Bill helped the woman thoroughly search her barn and tool shed, but found nothing. He suggested that maybe my gold detector could comb the grounds.

I went along with that by asking, "What's in it for me?"

"She promised me a grand. I'll go you halves if you find it," Bill offered.

I asked the obvious: "How big is her property?"

"Ten acres, the same as mine," he said.

"Alright, I'm in." I saw no point in wasting time. "When do we do it?"

++++

A week later, I swept the paddocks with the detector tuned to that soil type, with headphones on. A total waste of time and effort I thought the moment I got started, with every third or fourth step taken locating bits of roofing iron, fence staples, rusted metal and short lengths of discarded wire. No signal could be ignored because the cash box was known to be made of tin. With Bill digging, it progressed quickly once we established a pattern. If the earth was compacted, we left it; and if it was soft, he dug; eventually that evening only the fenced-out compound remained unsearched. I had combed the paddocks first to eliminate any doubt later that the cash box might be somewhere out there. If it existed anywhere on the property, it must lie hidden within the compound. I had no doubt about that, and promised to return and finish the job the next day.

The moment the detector coil swept the ground at the rear of the house, I knew we had problems: metal trash through the years had mineralised the soil, rendering the detector virtually useless. After fitting a small coil for pinpoint tracking, it still could not localise the signal. I explained the problem.

Bill wanted me to persist; otherwise we had wasted two days. To satisfy him, I did a half-hearted search of the flowerbeds, veggie garden, and both rows of agapanthus lining the driveway. Reasonable signals convinced me that nothing as large as a cash box lay buried there. With only the barn's perimeter remaining unsearched, the owner of the property, Nora, came with us to help. Bill tried unsuccessfully to dissuade her, but she said a nervy mare in there would need calming.

At least around the barn the detector had a chance – long wooden beams with a rammed-earth floor, no metal in its construction except for the roofing iron and large galvanised bolts used to secure the frame. The only other concentration of metal was the nails in the flooring of the mezzanine floor where hay bales and saddles were stored. A steel frame would have blanketed the coils field making any signal from the cash box indistinguishable from the surrounding metal, and the box would never have been located.

Yeah, we found it. Squeezed in under a floor beam from outside, with soil kicked over it: not even hidden really, but invisible to anyone searching without a metal detector. Nora was there, in on the find . . . and just as well for her. Locked or not, Bill would have had it open in a moment, and *we* would have visited the storage place intent on learning what his neighbour had left behind.

+ + + +

I did a job for a sawmill manager by running my gold detector over the butts of twenty or so logs stacked at the rear of his lumber yard, to locate and mark metal in them. Two had wire protruding from the cambium (the trees had probably grown next to a fence) but the remainder had malicious damage, done by stupid greenies who hammered in large nails in an attempt to prevent harvesting of the trees. A circular saw-blade at the mill had hit one and shattered into pieces, slicing a mill worker's hand, arm, and face: a near-death incident. The entire load of logs from that district had to be set aside and remain unmilled. Hearing of the accident when buying timber, I offered my services as a solution for a small fee.

The manager voiced doubt of accepting my offer untested: he challenged me to prove the efficacy of the detector on their garishly-painted outdoor table by locating and marking the location of screws driven in from underneath. When I was finished, he crawled beneath the tabletop and confirmed that I had identified every screw. He built the table, he proudly said, and the demo had convinced him. I got the job.

+ + + +

Bill queried if I thought a pistol stashed in a house could be located using a metal detector. (Police protocols called for detector use during weapon searches.) He obviously worried that a police raid might uncover his gun, and sought my opinion. I replied that an experienced operator trained to recognise anomalies in a variety of environments knew what to expect and would easily detect a firearm concealed under a floorboard or in a wall cavity, due to the massive amount of metal involved.

If I may inject a comment of my own here, there are a surprising number of misleading signals and dangers for the unwary applying a metal detector in a building, revealed to me when conducting a search out of curiosity in a known environment. I built my own home, so I virtually know the placement of every nail and piece of electrical wiring throughout the structure. Yet the density of wooden beams, tiles and electrical wiring collectively confused the ear and mind to the point where I became befuddled. It took me a week of practice to interpret what each signal meant and that was my own place! Imagine the tragedy in a rushed house search with the power board still on, when a jemmy-bar meets electricity: a visit to the hospital if not the morgue would be very likely.

While speaking of this, Bill's smile grew, so I suspected he already knew what I covered and had considered it. "If you think your fridge motor is a good spot," I stabbed in the dark, "then guess again. Every cop knows that one." His smile faded.

"Whereas your shed, built completely of steel, would scramble a signal and even the concrete slab has double reo in it."

He reached into his pocket and pulled out a coin; then flipped it to me. It was an Australian Koala – a $200 coin. "Would it find that in the house?" he asked. "It's got ten grams of gold in it."

My answer was a hedged one. "Depends on where it's been hidden, and if in with all your knick-knacks, obviously not." (Bill had half-a-dozen antique display cases, filled with many old things made of metal that had caught his eclectic fancy, most of them valuable.)

"And what if it was outside somewhere?"

"Again, it would depend on what other metal is in the same vicinity. When burying a stash, most scatter junk metal in the hole as they backfill to confuse."

"If I hid this in the garden, do you think you could find it?"

"You know most of the tricks," I chided. "And it would take forever to search." I knew there was more to these questions than idle curiosity.

"Then what fucking good is a gold detector?" he sneered.

"A lot of good if used in gold-bearing country searching for gold nuggets like it's designed to do, "I laughingly replied. "Not in suburbia."

Bill was pursuing a devious path to money, so I asked what he expected of a gold detector, hoping he might be more open.

He stood up and walked to his back door. "Come to the shed," he said.

After entering through where a roller-door should have been (the building was open to the elements) I made a quick judgement. The amount of tools strewn on benches lining the walls, odd pieces of dismantled furniture stacked about, with shelving on the verge of collapse under the weight of a miscellany of bits-and-pieces of electrical goods and motorbike parts, I conceded immediately: "A metal detector would overload and go berserk in here."

"I figured that," he said with a sigh of regret in his voice. Maybe that was why he gave up on keeping his idea secret and finally revealed what he had in mind.

"I know someone who avoids tax and keeps his black money handy. He came up with fifteen grand in the middle of the night three months ago." I nodded to keep him going. "Not for me, but for a mate who pinched a tractor for him."

The picture was becoming clear. It had to be a dodgy cleanskin, a 'straight' who kept his slate clean by hiring criminals to break the law and do his dirty work. Bill would never target a staunch crim. I asked, "Why gold?"

"I bought a piece (handgun) from him six months ago; I paid for it with ten Koalas."

Now it made sense, so I asked, "And he has a shed filled with junk like you, I presume?" I could now see where this was headed.

"It's alarmed better than his house."

"Do you think that's where his stash is at?"

Bill smiled before elaborating. "With a stolen tractor and farm implements stored inside." The perfect metal environment to conceal something wanting to stay lost.

"No gold detector, or any detector for that matter," I confidently stated, "could locate gold coins concealed in what you describe." We stayed on the subject and worried it a bit, until I spotted a piece of orange pottery sitting on a shelf above where Bill stood. Its bright colour and perfect glaze immediately focused my interest. I asked him if he knew who manufactured it, suspecting what it might be.

"Dunno; there's no maker's mark on it. Just a milk jug I picked up somewhere. There's a red cup and saucer behind it."

Refraining from saying more, aware not to alert him that I suspected the jug might be vintage Fiesta-ware or uranium glass, as sometimes called, I lifted them down from the shelf. Uncertain of their age (date of manufacture determines price) I offered him $20 for the three pieces saying they would look good on a mantelpiece at my place.

"You can have them," he obligingly said as he walked out the shed.

I raced the articles to my car before Bill could reconsider and change his mind. A piece of Fiesta-ware made in the 30's would be worth hundreds. To confirm if I was right, a device called a Gamma Scout sat waiting in a drawer at home; all it needed was a fresh 9-volt battery. I bought one going home.

+ + + +

Walking a path through the park opposite Melbourne Airport, I headed towards the lookout point used by hundreds of visitors each month, a single granite outcrop high on a hill overlooking an historic homestead, with a 360 degree vista. An hour spent there searching with my detector paid off: a few coins richer, plus a near-new brass compass in a leather cover located in long grass nearby.

A half-hour after that, at another likely site amidst small granite boulders where a life-size metal horse had been erected cut from four-millimetre steel plate and painted black, the detector registered the first find of hundreds in that area: a pre-decimal silver coin. Two hours later, a small shoulder bag that normally carried the gold detector's spare battery pack and a drink bottle hung filled to the brim with silver coins. Satisfied that I had combed every square metre and with pockets bulging, I resembled a pokies winner as I headed back to my car.

I asked myself, why so many coins were strewn in a narrow arc covering an area up to fifty metres out. Randomly thrown and not accidently spilt in a pile or lost in a line from a bag with a hole as one might surmise. It remains beyond solution for me, and no coin was dated later than 1950.

That lucky find had triggered a memory of a hectic night in South Australia, more than a decade before, when I hastily buried a damaged cash box containing a few hundred dollars worth of coins and a dozen pieces of shattered raw opal taken from a safe I had blown, with police in hot pursuit less than an hour behind. I pocketed only notes and nothing else from that mangled safe to incriminate me if apprehended before reaching Adelaide. I never did return and dig up that box to recover the bits of valuable opal.

I remembered and easily located the distinctive corner fence-assembly where I had buried it, on the fringe of a sheep station out in the boondocks, but after repeated searches and review of memory, I had to conclude another prospector most likely had found it. That shit me! However, not all was wasted.

The real purpose of my travel was to visit a shop in Adelaide that sold every variety of mineral in Australia. Over the phone, I detailed the exact kind of uranium I sought. The proprietor said he had none of that quality in stock but knew a local fossicker who definitely owned a few radioactive chunks and would part with one for the right price. Rather than haggle and end up with an inferior piece, I offered $100 for a perfect specimen: ten times what a small piece of uranium would normally be worth. He assured me it would be in his shop within a few days. To not waste those days, I had gone prospecting for the stolen cash box.

At the rear of the shop, he showed me four bits of uranium in a crudely-made lead box. He knew I wanted a strong emitting piece, and therefore kept these in lead to stop the higher concentration of gamma rays. My Gamma Scout (the one used to confirm the glassware Bill gave me) was the size of a mobile phone – but if needed, I could borrow from a friend an industrial Geiger counter used in his scrap-metal yard. It had a telescopic sensor-arm one metre long. If the Scout detected emissions out to a distance of one metre, then the industrial counter, designed to register extremely low concentrations of radiation, would detect unobstructed gamma rays at twice that range.

Natural occurring uranium, called pitchblende before its atomic properties became known, has radium in it, extracted during the early twentieth century to make glow-in-the-dark luminous paint, used to light up aircraft instruments, clock-face dials, and even wristwatch hands before its cancer-causing effect became evident. Radiation devices exist all around us, and are used daily by industry. Gamma ray emitters, used to confirm the integrity of aircraft welds, and detect hidden flaws in high-pressure pipes before installation, are common. Smoke detectors, found in almost every home, need a tiny piece of radioactive americium to function.

The presence of radiation in old glassware or glaze confirms its value as a piece worth collecting. Long before the discovery of gamma rays at the start of the twentieth century, the waste product left after extracting radium from pitchblende became an excellent medium in glaze making: it caused minerals to combine and flow well. By the end of the twentieth century (where this story lives), the invisible gamma ray emissions coming from the glaze are readily detectable. My Scout had chirruped like a cricket as I moved it over the orange jug and the red cup and saucer. It confirmed for me, better than a pottery expert on Antiques Road Show, that they were real Fiesta-ware of a vintage collectors killed for, probably manufactured during the 1920 American flapper era.

During verification of the wares, I underwent a light-bulb moment; it bloomed complete as a solution to Bill's conundrum. It motivated me to kill two birds with one stone: obtain a piece of uranium and unearth a flattened cash box.

The second I never got, but the uranium was scary to begin with. The first two chunks of mineral tested at the shop left me unimpressed, but the moment my Scout ventured near the third piece, it triggered the speaker. I moved a metre away from the stone, and it still chirruped like mad! Australian-mined uranium is the best in the world and sought by developed countries, so concentrated that a relatively simple industrial process purifies it ready for use in nuclear reactors. So I have heard.

The piece I returned with to Melbourne was about the size of a square of chocolate (quite small) but it was so potent it scared me, this invisible seething danger lurking there in its little lead container in the boot as far from me at the steering wheel as I could put it!

I told Bill of my idea, and how it might work, but not in fine detail, and asked if I could borrow the Koala coin. He stressed a bit over the request, but finally said, "Nah, it's gone. But I've got a Rand." (A Kruger Rand is a South African coin, hoarded as a gold equivalent; 97% gold, with 3% copper which gives them their distinctive reddish colour.)

"Great! Give it to me." I was anxious to test my theory, and any gold coin would do.

The painful look he pulled caused me to laugh, and say, "You're not going to lose it. I just want to *borrow* one for a while."

After more talk, when finally I had him convinced, he suggested I should drive to the local pub and pick up a six-pack. (Bill trusted me with the whereabouts of his stash about as much as I trusted him with mine.)

When I returned to Bill's place, he climbed from his car in the carport as though he had just driven in before me. He may have been somewhere and returned, but I doubt it: when touching the bonnet in passing it felt cold. Inside the house, he handed me a small lilac plastic cube – a coin-collector's display container clipped shut – and asked, "Will that do?"

When opened, it pleased me to see an uncirculated one-ounce Kruger Rand, elevated on a clear-plastic saddle for ease of viewing, with a perfect cavity, as though made for my experiment, beneath the coin for the concealment of the uranium.

I left him so fast to get back to my place and affix the uranium and borrow the Geiger counter, I am sure he thought I was doing a runner on him the way he stared at my pocket where the Rand sat snug out of sight. "I'll be back in a couple of hours," I reassured him. Excited to test my theory, I drove in a beeline for home.

+ + + +

To put the danger of radiation poisoning in perspective, risk is proportional to dose, over time. General accepted theory is that the hour spent by me shaping the piece of uranium to fit the cavity beneath the coin irradiated my hands and face with less radiation than exposing them to one hospital X-ray: and eight

X-rays over a twelve-month period would cause no lasting harm.

Later that evening back at Bill's place, I handed him the plastic box. "Hide that somewhere in your shed," I advised him. "But don't shove it under a plate of steel or in your safe. This is just an experiment."

He peered at the uranium, trying to suss what I had glued there, oblivious to the fact of his face being bombarded with thousands of gamma rays per second. He would have flung it at me in heathenish fright if I had told him.

Out to the shed he went, while I waited anxiously with the borrowed Geiger counter switched on and clicking away, the needle on the dial flickering, registering the ambient radiation in his house. The moment he returned from the shed, I sped out past him. A disappointing five-minute preliminary circuit inside the shed got no result. Still convinced my idea would work, I settled down and commenced a methodical search for the uranium, and within ten minutes I located it concealed under a bench amidst a half-dozen salvaged starter motors. (Bill wrongly assumed the thick metal and copper windings would stymie the Geiger counter as it would a gold detector.) When I returned with a smile of victory on my face bearing the coin-container in hand, Bill was beside himself and all over me with praise demanding that I explain to him how I did it.

✛ ✛ ✛ ✛

That same week Bill organised the purchase of another piece, and when collected the Kruger Rand was included in the payment. Two nights later, that handgun travelled loaded with Bill and me to a property in western Victoria where a quarter-moon with clouds in the sky cast constantly moving shadows: ideal conditions for stealth and secretiveness as we crept in close to a farmhouse with outbuildings, and off to one side, a barn-like shed.

Our target was the shed (a house invasion would **never** be on our agenda) with a siren box and blue globe visible beneath the eaves. Bill knew how to disarm the alarm and only the house had a camera visible outside. Cropped pasture grass covered the surrounding area, and a gravelled well-worn track connected the shed to the house. While waiting for Bill to confirm that the shed alarm was active and doors locked (people often forget), I tuned the Geiger counter to its most neutral setting. The needle on the dial hovered just above zero, and the speaker gave a muted tweet every second or so.

Having almost completed a thorough outside sweep of the shed walls with the Geiger counter's arm fully extended so the sensor could search high – on the chance of pinpointing the whereabouts of a radiation leakage if one existed before breaking in – a rusted junk-filled utility chassis next to the shed on the side visible to the house blocked our way. Bill circled out in the moonlight, while I stayed in the shadow cast by the shed, and squeezed between it and the wreck. A 'cricket' began to chirp. My heart raced. Radiation detected! The chirruping sound from the small speaker sounded loud in the night. Hastily, I flicked the switch and killed the sound.

With just the glowing needle on the dial to go by, I waved the sensor over the shed. The needle previously near the middle of the dial had dropped to its lowest position. It disappointed me. I whispered to Bill, who had heard the 'cricket' and hurriedly returned, that it was obviously a false alarm; but as I spoke, the needle again moved up! By luck, the sensor at the end of the arm had swung around and was pointing in the direction of something radioactive in the engine-well of the wreck less than a metre from me, where a bonnet and motor should have been, but instead gaped open filled with used oil-filters, old hubcaps, and stripped-out wiring of every kind. Uncertain of success, and expecting disappointment, I switched the sound back on as I probed the sensor in deep amongst the rubbish. The 'cricket' arced up and went ballistic!

+ + + +

18
GOOD OIL

Smith and Wesson MP 40

ARROGANCE HINDERS INTELLECT

- Joe Tog

Serge was known around the traps as a person who could get stuff cheap. Stuff that fell off the back of a truck if you get my drift: a toaster, fry pan, television, or even a washing machine if you wanted one. Much cheaper than the prevailing price, if you were prepared to wait. When we first met I thought he was a fence for stolen goods (a Fagan who waits like a spider in the middle of a thieves' web) but I gradually learned that he had far more depth of character than that.

A tall man from one of those Eastern-bloc countries, athletic and very fit. He walked everywhere with a rucksack on his back and preferred public transport, or ran accompanied by his two dogs, a female Doberman always on his left and a frisky crossbreed that roamed twenty paces out in front.

Whenever I visited, the Doberman stood aloof and if Serge changed his position, she moved too. But the bitser always greeted me with a friendly bark and sat with tail wagging until the obligatory pat had been dispensed before wandering off to settle down on her mat in the kitchen. However, during one visit all of that changed.

The moment Serge opened his front door in response to my knock, the friendly nature of the bitser changed. She barked repeatedly and backed away from me the moment I stepped through the doorway into the hall. Serge was startled and the Doberman snarled in response to the bitsers barking, baring her teeth and before I could even begin to feel scared of the situation, Sedge growled, "Sit!"

Obedient, the Doberman sat, but continued to grumble in her throat.

"What's gotten into those two?" I asked, genuinely bothered by their reaction to me. I own dogs and always get on well with animals.

Serge closed the door before answering. "Nothing to worry over, mate," he said. "Let's go to the kitchen." His voice sounded strained and that made me feel slightly uneasy. As much unease as the bitser's sudden dislike of me.

I sat at the kitchen table while Serge went in search of the bitser with a treat, and throughout the remainder of the visit, I never laid eyes on her. The reason I dropped by was discussed and within ten minutes I had left, the dog's behaviour still unexplained. By the end of the week, I had forgotten it.

When next I visited a short time on, the bitser responded in exactly the same way. She yelped in fear and ran from me to another part of the house (the Doberman treated me with disdain) and when I tried to go after the bitser, Serge stopped me.

"Leave her, Joe." Then he added, "It's the way I want her to be."

It was a strange comment to make about a troubled dog, so I queried what he meant. "Why would you want a dog to be scared?"

"You haven't caused her to change. It's the way she is sometimes." I could hear the unspoken words loud and clear that he wanted me to drop it. So I did. However, I continued to think about her behaviour after leaving his place: something bad had traumatised her. I somehow had triggered it, but for the life of me, I could not work out what I had done. Sometimes I care less for people than I do for animals: next time at Serge's I intended to confront him and find out what it was that troubled her.

The bitser showed a friendly greeting as I entered, but would not venture nearer to me until I coaxed her over with kind words. After a pat and dubious sniffs, she was back to being her old self. In the kitchen, she calmly settled down on her mat, inferring the two previous visits had been an aberration and now forgotten. Either she was a fruitcake, or she had truly sensed something different about me during my last two visits. And for a variety of reasons her response seriously bothered me.

A fortnight later, I again dropped in on Serge. When the bitser ran to get a pat in response to my voice calling her, she stopped in mid-stride halfway up the passage and angrily barked at me before running away: that finally confirmed what I had suspected. It was an enlightening moment, supporting my belief that she was not schizoid.

Certain that I was right I broached the subject with Serge the moment we settled down in the kitchen with a beer each from his fridge. "Your dog's trained to smell a gun," I confidently stated, and waited for his response.

"No, she's not trained," Serge quickly said.

"I never carried one last time I dropped in, and she was friendly." I figured he was lying to me.

"No dog can smell a gun," he persisted.

"I've got this one I carried two weeks back." I pulled it from my pocket and showed him.

Not the least bit put-off by the small pistol in my hand he again said, "No dog can smell a gun."

"But I know she –"

"It's the gun-oil she smells," he cut me off. "Not the gun."

He played a semantic game: like denying he punched someone when accused of punching, when in fact he most definitely elbowed 'em!

"But I've been here before with a gun and she's never carried on like the last few times." I could not grasp the notion.

"Then you must have changed your oil," he matter-of-factly said.

And he was right about that, spot on! Only a month earlier I had traded my bulkier 32 Webley for a compact Browning 25 that came in a box with a small can of genuine gun-oil included. Up until then I had used Singer sewing machine oil. It worked fine and did as good a job at quarter the price.

"A friend owned her," Serge explained. "She bit a Jack and got kicked badly; the vet thought she would die. I suppose he over-oiled his gun that day; so now that particular oil-smell frightens her shitless." I earnestly reminded myself, there and then, to toss the genuine oil and return to using Singer.

We sat and talked, and covered subjects previously avoided. I felt closer to him now, knowing he had cared for the injured dog after its owner had been arrested. Serge was seriously bent and he told me he had been so for many years, but through a combination of luck and good management, he remained a cleanskin (an unconvicted law-breaker).

"Why do you want the dog to stay scared of gun-oil?" I asked, knowing if he answered honestly, it meant we had gone up a notch in mutual trust.

His answer, when it came, satisfied me that he had given it much thought. "Most police use the oil she hates: it's an expensive spray-on made by Remington. They get it at a discount." And he should know, being an expert in cut-price goods.

"If a Jack or an undercover is nearby, she runs away; all I do is look in the opposite direction to see who she's run from." He sipped his beer.

"And what about the Doberman?" I asked. "How does she fit in?" My memory fails me, and it is unclear now, as to how the conversation developed to the point of trust and disclosure, but by the end of that visit, Serge had divulged an unusual tale.

As a common practice in his country, Dobermans and Alsatians are posted as sentries on military buildings and used to patrol airfields and naval yards. They are alert and more reliable than human guards, making it less likely to be breached by a sneaky intruder. Serge resorted to using a similar tactic, slightly changed to advantage himself, the intruder! By running everywhere, he was training for getting away from, or getting to, a crime. He would post a reliable nit-keeper he could trust, the Doberman at the entrance into whatever place he intended to rob, along with the bitser running around and sniffing, doing her own thing.

Inside the building safely out of sight, Serge would fill his rucksack with goods, confident that his back was covered: unlike a human, a loyal dog will die for its master and he relied on that. Human lookouts often leave their associates for dead when least expected, and flee to save their own skin if confronted.

In one particular dicey situation he spoke of, the Doberman had been wounded slightly when shot by a security guard she had bailed up trying to enter a building in response to a silent alarm Serge had unknowingly tripped. As the shots rang out, Serge in flight pelted from the building's rear entrance. After a minute of running, he stopped and blew three blasts on an ultra-sonic whistle to call his dogs to him, then continued running, knowing the dogs would catch up.

Another time, the bitser saved him from a diet of porridge (doing time). She scratched frantically at a glass door she could see him through and sat looking about whining anxiously, but that was enough warning for Serge. He fled from the scene as though the hounds of hell pursued him, into the backyard and through a hole in the fence with the protective Doberman right behind him with the bitser following, only moments before the front door of his hide-out crashed in. Serge said he lost all of his belongings to the police that day, but the bitser had saved his freedom and that was most important to him. They camped in a national park for a week, and ate take-away every day until he found another suitable place to rent.

The next time the bitser warned Serge of oil, she indirectly helped someone else. When running, because the bitser roamed out in front, she reacted badly to a druggie slumped next to a tree on the nature-strip ahead. Serge had no reason to worry (his rucksack was empty) so warily ran past a person he would not normally bother to view suspiciously.

It was not until later he put the situation together and realised that an associate of his lived across the road from where the druggie sat. A cautionary phone call quickly followed to give a heads-up about the druggie lurking across the road, leaving out mention of the likelihood that he carried a gun. A day or two later a return 'thank you' call confirmed that his suspicions had been correct. Only more correct than expected. Two tattooed louts residing in that street, recruited to rough up the druggie and move him on, received a nasty surprise. They were arrested on the spot and taken away for questioning!

+ + + +

19
ARSON

Assorted oriental rugs

A CLEAR CONSCIENCE IS USUALLY THE SIGN OF A CONVENIENT MEMORY

Floor coverings are expensive, especially hand-woven rugs and mats. I learnt that early in life. Carpets vary in value depending on the budget, and their price can range from a modest sum up to and exceeding the ridiculous. A Middle Eastern guy (whose name I have long forgotten) taught me that by simply buying stolen mats and rugs from me at a quarter of their marked cost and then selling them just under the market value as legitimate imports through his own shop. The expensive traceable ones were sold 'under the counter' at half price without a state tax levied.

Directing me to steal stock from other merchants' shelves

accomplished three things for him: it lessened competition, made more sales, and it reduced costly imports. Overall, he had a sweetheart deal with me and a few others keeping him supplied with floor coverings. I received a chance business education from a perspective not usually seen. However, like a lot who produce black money, he became greedy and wanted more. A competitor, profiting from the artificially-created shortage, needed stopping but he had an unbeatable security system that protected him from robbery (a family member lived above the shop). The solution was arson.

In the late 70s when asked to burn a shop, intuitively I knew that was a deviant crime best avoided. Those around me also declined, but eventually a crim from Sydney came down and did the job. (In prison during the early 80s where the captive situation obliged me to share an exercise yard with a few firebugs, they all seemed creepy and associated with the sex offenders and their ilk. However, the guy I met who burnt for money seemed a 'normal' criminal, akin to a burglar or a factory breaker.)

When this shop blazed as though incendiaries were inside, about five fire units fought the flames, and did it burn! When we heard in a newsflash that the place was an inferno a mate and I drove there to experience the fire scene and the person who lit it, along with the one who paid him, were parked there watching. (That proves the truth of the saying that the arsonist who lit the fire is usually in the crowd!) Without any hope of putting it out, before the building collapsed destroying every piece of competition stock, the fire fighters fought desperately to protect adjoining premises. Watching his opponent's shop burn perhaps is what sparked the idea in his head to have a second building burnt six months later.

His shop and storeroom, filled with recently imported expensive stock straight from England and Turkey, was undergoing renovations, but oddly in the cheapest way possible. During that time of closure, the new stock was swapped for less quality merchandise.

That confused me at first, but because I helped relocate the grouse carpets to his other shop in Sydney Road, Coburg, and stack damaged stock and rolls of old carpets that had been pulled up and returned for disposal into his storeroom, the type of activity quickly revealed the swindle. He intended to burn down his own shop!

He never confided his intentions to me, and most of the carpets stacked in the store were good, but old stock and out of fashion, along with about one third of the dodgy stuff. I did not need a Mensa IQ to work it out from that. In addition, a delivery of expensive paint arrived but none of it saw the light of day on the walls of his shop. I transferred the paint along with new light fittings, doors and such to the Coburg shop. An insurance fraud of which I worked on the periphery without needing to know about the inner details, except that the same arsonist turned up to do the job, and he liked to boast about what he did. Having an active curiosity along with a retentive memory, I remember how he did it.

According to the fire report for the insurance company, the newly fitted ceiling lights (the light fittings installed at the Coburg shop) attributed to the cause of the fire by requiring more electricity than the old wiring in the building could safely carry. Those facts, combined with other evidence, showed rats had gnawed wiring allowing live electrical wires to contact each other and cause a spark: rat bodies discovered in the ceiling, burnt beyond a crisp in the ash of newly installed insulation, confirmed the observation. Their known appetite for plastic directly caused the fire, and that is what the arson squad reported to the insurance company. However, I knew different.

The arsonist asked one of my associates to get him four movie reels (this is before DVDs, when a movie was a long strip consisting of tens of thousands of tiny pictures passing a light and projected onto a screen at thirty-two frames a second), but stipulated that he did not want them reported stolen. A crime report of that specificity just prior to a fire might alert the arson squad to investigate deeper into a less obvious cause. Made out of pure cellulose, film burns at an incredible rate and it leaves no visible residue. (Made from less pure cellulose, a ping-pong ball stinks when burning, but disappears at the same rate.)

Three reels of film were woven through the rolls of stacked carpet to accelerate their burning, bought from an usher who pilfered them from the storage room of the Padua Theatre where he worked. A fourth roll unreeled in the ceiling guaranteed that the spark generated by the 'rat-gnawed' wires instantly took hold in the insulation, becoming unstoppable by the time the first fire unit arrived in response to the alarm.

+ + + +

Sharing a shout of drinks with a few of us in the know, while waiting for a taxi to take him to Essendon Airport for his flight back to Sydney, the arsonist told of three jobs he had done overseas. Two were devious paybacks, so insurance was not the intention – the exact opposite actually – intended to punish through the pocket, by voiding any insurance claim.

The first job involved a radiant heater of which all householders know the danger: the bar type which uses electrical resistance to heat a wire element coiled round and along a ceramic insulator. Hanging a damp jacket over the back of a chair to dry out in front of one is common on a wet day when nothing will dry, or left to dry overnight. In every example a disaster waiting to happen once the clothing dries when radiant heat often sets things alight. When this is proven, insurance companies invariably refuse payment.

Hired for this particular nasty, while the occupants were out enjoying a movie, he broke in and searched until he found a radiator and a clothes-horse as well as a hand-full of undies taken from a bedroom dresser. With the radiator tipped frontward and the undies-covered clothes-horse collapsed on top, he had set the scene exactly as he wanted an arson team to construe it. (*Everyone* at some time has dried underwear in front of a heater.) After repairing the jemmied window to hide where he had entered, and before leaving by the front door, he plugged in the radiator and switched it on. He was in his car two streets away when the carpet reached ignition point and burst into flame. The local brigade responded to his Samaritan call reporting smoke billowing from beneath the eaves of a house – the evidence of negligence needed finding so that the insurance claim would fail – and he watched the promptly-dispatched fire crew smash in the front door and save the property. The cost of repairing the damage had to come out of the victim's own pocket.

+ + + +

The second incident was set up in such a way that it would make the victim, a building inspector, believe that an attempt on his life had narrowly failed when a device capable of killing misfired. A scheming builder, opposed by the victim, wanted him to believe after the incident that he had escaped death by a freak piece of luck (the investigating police report later confirmed it), making him mentally amenable to what the builder sought.

He had to believe that someone in the building industry was definitely out to get him, so that when approached by the builder offering sympathy and help he would agree to allow an irregularity or two. In return, the builder's tough associates would pretend to track down the threat before a repeat attempt and make it go away.

The inspector made jewellery as a hobby in his backyard shed, and had a powerful globe in a desk lamp mounted to the workbench to illuminate his work. On this particular evening when he went out to his shed for relaxation, the fluorescent lights hanging from the ceiling lit up perfectly after he entered and switched them on. However, at the bench his powerful work-light refused to illuminate, even though I can imagine he flicked the switch on and off a half dozen times in frustration. It was not until he unscrewed the globe to inspect the filament that he saw it half-filled with liquid and smelt a whiff of petrol in the air. He fled the shed in rampant fright and called the police immediately.

A forensic report confirmed that if the wall socket had not been faulty, the perfectly good filament inside the light would have glowed for a split second before it burnt, turning the petrol into an incandescent ball of expanding flame. (The argon gas inside the light bulb to prevent the filament from burning would have seeped out via the hypodermic hole that introduced the petrol.) Of course, the wall plug was never faulty until made so by the arsonist.

+ + + +

The third crime he described doing was so straightforward that a few years earlier I had done exactly what he did to burn a place down: not intentionally, but through dumb-arse ignorance! My mum's old electric iron, given to me when I needed one, often blew the fuse in my flat, so one day, thinking myself clever, I solved the problem by replacing the thin fuse wire with a length of thick copper wire stripped out of an old electrical cord.

What I did not know then, but quickly realised with dawning awareness as I listened to his story unfold, was that a fuse wire is purposely thin and *meant* to burn through and instantly stop the flow of electricity to a faulty appliance that triggered it in the first instance. Each time the ironing cord twisted in a certain way the wires inside the cord would touch, causing resistance that instantly heated the fuse and blew it. But when the substituted fuse is thick copper wire, the outcome is reversed so that the electricity keeps flowing and heats the thinner wiring in the cord until the covering bursts into flame. Fortunately, in that same period I bought a new iron cheap (it fell off the back of a delivery truck) so the copper wire in the fuse holder faded from memory.

Not until hearing that a thick fuse wire neutralised the safety feature of a circuit breaker, turning any fault in the electrical wiring of a house, or an appliance, into a ticking time bomb did I realise that the flat I once rented may have burnt down years before because of my lack of knowledge about electricity.

+ + + +

20
BY MANY MEANS

Sea container

NEVER HANG ON TO YOUR PAST:
IT WILL CLOUD THE VISION OF YOUR FUTURE

My sister returned from a Bali holiday, espousing praise of the
Balinese people, along with two carved wooden elephants she
intended to sit on her bookshelf. The moment she displayed them
alarm bells rang loud in my head. I grabbed one and tipped it over
to study the bottom. Glued there was a piece of black material
bearing the manufacturer's name. I peeled it off, shocking my
sister into grabbing the elephant back from me. I picked up and
did the same to her other one. It took an hour to convince my
sister that drugs are smuggled into the country using innocent
victims as unpaid, unwitting mules. She was adamant that the

carvings stayed in her locked room at the resort for the duration of the vacation; nothing like I suggested could have happened.

Depending on where the resort is located, and who is employed in the right position, or does the cleaning, once the identity of the carving's owner and place of abode is established in Australia, a carving is switched for a more sinister one: steamed and sterilised, sealed with wax, it travels openly to a known destination, in this case, fortunately, not my sister's. The elephant I saw lay smashed in pieces in a rubbish bin, along with a miscellany of other stolen property taken during a burglary in Bendigo to make it appear as a legit robbery if the burglar was nabbed in a police stake-out.

+ + + +

A hardnosed Sydney criminal, who later became the suspect for a handful of unsolved murders, started a business repairing damaged shipping containers for overseas customers. Like often happens with a business that goes dodgy, it started out legitimately with good intent, then, as a hidden potential of the business was recognised, a scam is introduced.

Border security (customs) can only search a small number of the thousands of containers unshipped at Australian wharves every month of the year. And because those containers needing repair arrive from every country, and not just the known drug routes, it becomes impossible to keep track of them all. The entire system for intercepts functions on information gathered from informers and other sources of intelligence. Without informers to keep customs advised, the system fails.

In this scam the container, not its contents, concealed the contraband. This repairman operated on the principal that if only two knew about it then it would remain a secret provided the other person was dead. All he sees now is the six sides of a prison cell while serving two cumulative life sentences, and not a container in sight.

His current accomplice at the time, this one still within his used-by date and alive, did a stitch-up deal with police to save his own neck on another criminal matter by disclosing the A to Z on how the empty container scam worked. The police, once alerted to his activities, backtracked and unravelled the rest, including the previously unknown murder count.

+ + + +

An enterprising criminal who grew up in Perth bought a small trawler and branched into the pelagic fishing business. No big-deal kind of thing but eventually, through vessels met at sea from Afghanistan, it led to smuggling. For three years, together with his fishing aspirations and crew of two, Ian traded an assortment of 'fenced' Australian merchandise (some of it sold to him by me) for bootleg products such as alcohol, music cassettes, porno (this occurred in the late 70s) electronic goods, and every so often an illegal immigrant. It earned him a steady income but not sufficient to retire on. So when an American associate in Brisbane proffered a one-off deal that would solve all of his current financial problems – ten bales of prime quality Afghanistan marijuana in a single consignment to be his next Indian Ocean pick-up – he jumped at the opportunity. And by providing the transport and half of the finance, six bales would be his.

One month later in Australian waters after three weeks at sea, the glowing buildings of Perth's CBD in morning sunrise cloaked a fast-approaching Customs vessel until the last minute when it appeared out of nowhere and pulled alongside the returning trawler. Unknown to Ian the confiscated consignment later proved to consist of poor grade marijuana (not high grade as expected) with a knelling package of opium stashed inside one of the bales. Being the owner of the trawler, Ian in due course was convicted and because of the opium, which carried a heavier penalty than Mary Jane, a sentence of twelve years in prison was handed down.

(As the passing of time and loose lips revealed years after this event, unknown to Ian then, the American had been using delaying tactics in court to oppose his deportation back to the USA as a *persona non grata*, and he was becoming desperate. The legal eagles on the case predicted he would lose, when abruptly the crown application ceased. The opium had obviously been put there by an Afghani accomplice at the behest of the Yank when he organised the load, to make Ian appear to be a bigger fish than he was. History showed that the Yank had formulated sufficient 'facts' to barter a reprieve.)

+ + + +

Like boats and trains, aeroplanes require regular maintenance but there are some nefarious people who speed the process up for their own gain. During a long flight from Italy to Melbourne, a passenger unbolted a couple of seat-belts and left them under a blanket where they were soon discovered by a cleaning crew after everyone had alighted. (Passengers regularly move to empty seats to nap during long flights on a plane.) While the aircraft was refuelled for its next flight the airport's maintenance crew were assigned to check every seat-belt in the plane.

During the aircraft check one of the maintenance guys used the toilet, which is a no-no when a plane is on the ground. His workmates criticised him for it – they suggested he was avoiding work – until he sheepishly admitted he had diarrhoea caused by a party he attended the night before. After a few friendly jibes, it was quickly forgotten.

The seat-belt incident was logged as an in-flight act of random vandalism, and the plane was given the all-clear. What the airline authorities missed by the diversion is what was in that toilet, cleverly concealed behind a panel during the international flight: two packets which customs would love to have seized. Not narcotics as one might first suspect, but a hundred tiny glass phials filled with a life-saving miracle drug called Interferon banned in Australia (until approved in the 90s) at the time more valuable to the consignee than heroin, undetected by the trained dogs earlier let loose in the plane by customs officers, to sniff out the regular type of illicit drugs.

+ + + +

Singapore is a clean country with an even cleaner capital city. Heavy fines exist for anyone foolish enough to publicly litter. And look out, anyone caught spitting in the street! Car fumes cannot be avoided, but the one thing I am certain you will not have seen, if you went there in the 80s, is chewing gum on the footpath, or for sale in a shop. It was a forbidden substance equal to an import such as marijuana, though the penalty was not as harsh, but nevertheless totally banned from the island. (The Prime Minister of Singapore must have stepped on a gob of gum in the street at sometime. How else could good old chewy become an enemy of the state?)

But seriously, if a packet of chewing gum was found by Customs in a traveller's pocket or suitcase at the airport, it was as though a heinous crime had been detected. And the very least a visitor underwent was a severe tongue lashing about the evils of gum, along with the offending gum thrown into the rubbish bin. And knowing when a prohibition law existed, money could be earned from it, an enterprising mate of mine smuggled thousands of packets into that nation of elderly chewing gum addicts, introduced to gum as children by American soldiers during the Singapore occupation after WW2.

In the early 80s a packet of chewing gum cost 35c wholesale in Australia. But under the counter, in a Singapore outlet, the equivalent of $2.50 Australian was the black-market going rate! Seven times the gum's original value, and Jim (the guy who did it was a greedy bastard) broke in and pinched thousands of packets of PK, and every other kind of gum from corner shops, beach kiosks, school tuck-shops, and anywhere else that sold chewing gum, to avoid the 'costly' overheads of paying for it in the proper way.

+ + + +

In the 90s when Russia, formally known as the USSR, was the largest nation in the world, their most popular car was exported to a dozen or more countries. I bought one of them from a Lada dealership at Hoppers Crossing, just south of Melbourne towards Geelong. It was a robust four-wheel drive utility and I enjoyed touring around the countryside of Victoria even though most of my mates said it was a piece of shit! It had a crank handle in case the battery went flat, and a twelve-piece bag of tools stamped CCCP to fix it with if ever it broke down. And along with that, I knew a back-story to the Lada which endowed it with a secret which only a few were privy to.

The Russian government manufactured Ladas and had factories spread across the USSR making parts, but when it came to assembly only two plants did it. The western one near Moscow distributed them down highways into Europe and the other plant in the east shipped out of Vladivostok. And every couple of months a sea consignment of Lada cars would arrive at a Sydney wharf. When ordering mine, I had to wait nearly eight weeks because of the deep red colour ordered. It came direct from the USSR to me via the dealership.

I received a phone call telling me that my vehicle had finally arrived along with five others, delivered by a car-carrier direct from the Custom's compound in Sydney, but it would take a further two days for the dealership to detail it. Not happy with the delay, I was forced to wait until the weekend and then asked a mate to drive me down.

My red utility waited on the edge of the yard, and it looked so shiny and new! I could hardly wait to sign the paperwork. At the desk I noticed that the roller door in the side of the dealership had been damaged and so I asked, "What happened there?"

"Some bastard broke in last night," the salesman said.

"What did they steal?" I queried, thinking there can't be much to pinch from a dealership.

"Nothing seems to be gone," he admitted. "But why bust in and throw everything out of the filing drawers – it pisses me off!"

To change his mood, I asked, "Where are the other Ladas you said were delivered?" I wanted to look them over.

"Three were picked up yesterday by customers. My detailer finished your car last night. They must have broken in straight after he locked up." The robbery had really annoyed him.

"So that's why I had to wait two days," I coldly stated: "Why me, why not make one of them wait?"

He immediately went into damage control, soothing an unhappy customer, giving me two extra rubber floor-mats and an air freshener. I drove away happy. About seven months later I found out why the break-in had occurred.

Sam, an Albanian mate who persistently tried to convert me to communism, explained it all one day when he came down from

Sydney to visit. Not the fine detail of how it was done, or who was involved other than they were his cronies, but the gist of it. The frame in a Lada is constructed out of square tube, and cannot be easily inspected (so I was told). A perfect place to conceal contraband, and on the eastern seaboard of the Soviet Republic that is exactly what happened.

The USSR manufactured a massive amount of military firearms for sale worldwide, particularly automatic Kalashnikov rifles and semi-automatic pistols, but unfortunately the Russian people at the same time had a nationwide food shortage. Pistols were filched from assembly lines and sold for a thousand roubles on the street to any local criminal who sought one. I never learned if my sturdy car played a part in the smuggling scam, but nevertheless I like the idea of thinking it did!

When cars are exported overseas they are transported direct from the car manufacturer to a security yard near the wharves where every nook and cranny of a vehicle is searched by customs and then guarded from theft until shipped. On arrival at the destination country they are again searched, usually not as thoroughly, with dogs sniffing for the odour of drugs that may have been stashed after the vehicles were loaded. The key that unlocked that heavily guarded Customs yard for criminals who stealthily entered one night is they were not there to steal a vehicle! They were there to stash things made of steel inside five of them.

Why pay fifteen grand in Australian money for six pistols, when Sam's crew knew, for ten grand's worth of quality Australian food packed into a sea-container and shipped to compatriots in Russia, they could get their hands on better weapons and also recoup their original costs by importing a few extra pistols for sale in Australia? A win-win situation if ever I have heard of one.

While the unwitting security guards kept vigil at the gates, ten handguns (two per car) were cunningly concealed inside the steel chassis that a Lada is built around. Three mainland states in Australia each had one Lada dealership back then – most of the vehicles stayed in NSW after being unloaded, while a few were trucked north to Queensland and the remainder travelled south to Victoria – so it was easy to enter three car yards and search until they located what was theirs. Unfortunately a few of the cars were picked up earlier than predicted by customers in Melbourne, before they could be liberated of what they carried: hence the break-in to get the addresses from the purchase forms. To my knowledge they were not caught.

+ + + +

According to a news report released by the Victorian homicide squad – after an extensive investigation – an innocent woman had been mistakenly murdered and police were seeking assistance from the public to help apprehend those responsible. The rumour I heard five years later was that her murder was no mistake. She had been cunningly deceived into secretly lending money to purchase untaxed jewellery believing it would return triple her outlay, and was then knocked off by her 'partner in crime' before she revealed her clever deal to anyone. And the jewellery may only have existed in the mind of her callous murderer. Every decision we make is a gamble of one kind or another.

+ + + +

AUSSIE TRUE CRIME STORIES

Joe Tog

ISBN 9781922175373		Qty
RRP	AU$24.99	.....
Postage within Australia	AU$5.00	.....
	TOTAL* $_____	

* All prices include GST

Name:..

Address: ....

....

Phone:...

Email: ....

Payment: ❑ Money Order ❑ Cheque ❑ MasterCard ❑ Visa

Cardholders Name:...

Credit Card Number: ....

Signature:..

Expiry Date: ....

Allow 7 days for delivery.

Payment to: Marzocco Consultancy (ABN 14 067 257 390)
PO Box 12544
A'Beckett Street, Melbourne, 8006
Victoria, Australia
admin@brolgapublishing.com.au

BE PUBLISHED

Publish through a successful publisher.
Brolga Publishing is represented through:
• **National** book trade distribution, including sales,
marketing & distribution through **Macmillan Australia.**
• **International** book trade distribution to
    • The United Kingdom
    • North America
    • Sales representation in South East Asia
• **Worldwide e-Book distribution**

For details and inquiries, contact:
Brolga Publishing Pty Ltd
PO Box 12544
A'Beckett St VIC 8006

Phone: 0414 608 494
markzocchi@brolgapublishing.com.au
ABN: 46 063 962 443
(Email for a catalogue request)